ANOF

A true story by Anna Paterson

Anorexia nervosa imprisoned me for twenty years of my life. Towards the end of my illness I weighed only 4 stones 10 lbs. (66 lbs.) and was close to death in intensive care.

When all hope was lost, a miracle came along which enabled me to re-join the human race. I know of very few anorexics who slipped so far down, for so long and had the good fortune to come back.

I hope this book serves as a lesson for others and helps those less fortunate, who are still in the clutches of Anorexia nervosa.

At birth, none of us have Anorexia nervosa.

WHAT IS ANOREXIA NERVOSA?

Before I tell you my life story, let me explain what Anorexia nervosa is and how it feels to have this illness. Why does a person become anorexic? How is the sufferer affected mentally and physically? And what exactly is this inner voice that controls all anorexics?

Anorexia nervosa is not an illness about dieting. Weight loss is involved but this is only a symptom of a much larger problem. The sufferer has low self-esteem and wants to disappear completely. Anorexics see thinness as the solution to all their problems. Anorexics believe they are unlovable and think that if they become thin, people will love them.

As the anorexics weight falls and they begin to starve, their mind focuses entirely on food. Although constantly hungry, the anorexic must avoid eating at all costs. An anorexics self-image is very distorted and, looking in a mirror at themselves, even when they are skin and bone, they see a body covered in fat. Being fat terrifies them.

All anorexics are controlled by an inner voice that dictates their every move. This voice in their heads forbids them food, telling them they do not deserve to eat. Anorexics believe they are bad people and as punishment starve themselves.

Anorexics assume they are to blame for everything. They consider themselves failures and often as an additional form of punishment, will start self-harming, such as cutting or burning themselves.

Their inner voice shouts loudly and persistently. *"You're fat! You're a worthless, fat, ugly pig! You're disgusting, revolting and hateful! Stop eating now! If you're thin everything will be alright."* It is this all powerful voice that keeps the sufferer in a life long anorexic state, threatening them that if they confide in anyone about this illness, they will be locked in a hospital and force fed until they're huge.

Anorexics are secretive and withdrawn and live in a world of fear. Petrified of becoming fat, they can never eat normally. Afraid to be a burden to others, they are unable to talk about their problems. As their weight drops the anorexics lose their powers of concentration. They can no longer sleep and become permanently restless. Anorexics frequently experience dizziness and fainting spells. For women, monthly periods stop altogether.

Once all the fat reserves have been used the anorexic's body feeds on its own muscles. The heart is all muscle and can soon become seriously damaged. This puts the anorexic at risk of a heart attack. Multiple organ failure is common in severe cases, as is reduction in bone density.

Over 90% of the cases of anorexia are linked to abuse. This abuse can range from severe mental or physical torment, to bullying and neglect. This neglect, this lack of love, usually occurs in the first ten years of an anorexics life. Anorexia nervosa is a slow suicide. The sufferer is imprisoned in a nightmare world of terror. Food is the enemy.

This is my story....

First published 2000 © Anna Paterson.
The right of Anna Paterson to be identified as the Author
of this work has been asserted by her in accordance with
the Copyright, Designs and Patents Act. 1988.

Published by Westworld International Limited,
London, England. 020 7823 1215

A CIP catalogue record for this book is available from
the British Library. ISBN 0-952-9215 2 9

Printed and bound by Mackays of Chatham, Kent.
Distributed by Central Books   020 8986 4854

1st printing September 2000
2nd printing March 2001
3rd printing September 2004

Poem – Slimmer on Trial by Robin Munro.
Printed on back page

**In this true story some names have been changed to
protect the innocent and preserve their privacy.**

I dedicate this book to

Simon

who has made my life

worth living.

I would like to thank my dear friend Mike Robeson, for all his help, encouragement and support and also Andy Pearson and Tracey Shellito for their time and help. In addition, both mine and Simon's parents, who have shown us much kindness throughout the writing of this book. I would like to thank Camille von Arnim and Stephen Smith for their hospitality, encouragement and guidance in putting this book together.

And finally I have to thank my Grandmother, without whom none of this would have been possible or necessary.

CONTENTS

Chapter	Page

HOW DOES AN INNOCENT CHILD GO
FROM THIS...

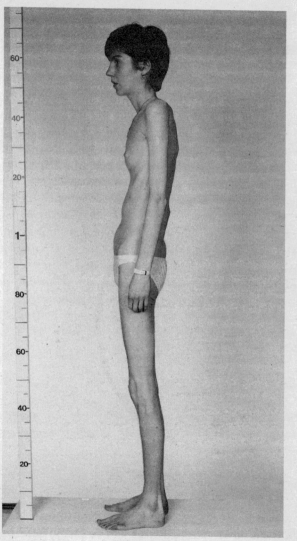

...TO THIS?

Chapter 1

CHILD ON ROUTE TO ANOREXIA NERVOSA

My name is Anna and I am anorexic. My story really begins with my first experience of child abuse at the age of three. It wasn't my parents or an older sibling or 'Uncle' who was abusing me, it was far more bizarre - it was my Grandmother. From the age of seven years old with my Mother addicted to tranquillisers I was imprisoned for long periods in my Grandmother's house. It was here the torment and force-feeding began. Constantly victimised by my Grandmother, as a teenager, I stopped eating in an attempt to disappear completely. By the age of 13, I was hospitalised and prescribed anti-depressants and barbiturates. These drugs were to draw me into a nightmare world of hallucinations where I lost the ability to read. As my anorexia became chronic I was admitted to intensive care where, weighing just 4 stone 10 lbs. (66 lbs.), I was close to death.

I survived where so many others haven't.

Why did this happen to me? Why are an increasing number of young people slowly starving themselves to death?

Perhaps my story has the answers.

I was born in 1968 in Southend, an English seaside town. We lived down the road from my Grandmother. To the outside world everything looked so normal, a happy young family, Mum, Dad, my two-year-older brother

Mark and now a little baby girl. A family who were lucky to have their Gran living so close. No one suspected that this short, plump, grey-haired, friendly old woman would turn out to become a malicious child abuser. The vicious torment from my Grandmother was to make me critically ill.

We were all scared of Gran, a compulsive control freak who ruined the lives of our entire family. Maybe my Grandmother's obsession to control everybody started when fate dealt her a blow earlier in her own life. She was widowed at the age of 32 during the war when her husband died of Tuberculosis, leaving her to bring up two little kids on her own. The same year Gran's sister, whose husband had deserted her, died, adding two more children to take care of. Over the years Gran's self-pity fermented into a hatred for the whole world, especially towards the lucky women with husbands and a wage coming in. It was this deep-seated bitterness that drove my Grandmother to control the people around her and ruin the lives of so many.

There were major problems with my Grandmother when Mum decided to marry Dad. Gran was against Dad and the marriage from the start. Mum getting married represented nothing but another betrayal. Her daughter, who she had striven so hard to bring up, was now abandoning her for a husband. With her uncanny ability to inflict guilt on us, she made my parents include her in practically everything they ever did. In many ways Dad married two women - Mum and Gran.

My Mum was a very feminine woman. She was tall, thin and pretty and worked on and off as an infant school teacher. Dad was an intelligent and good-looking man who worked as a forensic scientist for Scotland Yard in London. I remember there were times when they both seemed very happy and deeply in love, Dad always treating Mum with extreme kindness. But that wasn't allowed to last. My Grandmother was very into mind games, always playing one person off against another. My Father, who didn't possess a university degree in spite of his good job, was continually teased about the people Gran knew who had degrees. It was all said to undermine his confidence. He felt hurt and angry every time she mentioned degrees. Dad was very capable in most areas of his work; in fact he designed the original DNA database.

In other areas however, my Father was easily intimidated. For example, as a forensic scientist he found it impossible to appear and speak in court. It was too much for him to talk publicly or be cross-examined. He seemed unable to assert himself and always avoided any form of confrontation. It was this side of Dad that enabled Gran to rule his life from the beginning. My Father wasn't a bad person - he wasn't a child molester or a wife beater. He was merely someone who was totally intimidated by Gran, to the point where he was too frightened to challenge the obvious fact that his daughter's Grandmother was making his child ill. In Mum and Dad's defence, when my Grandmother hit me, leaving red marks on my legs, I would always lie saying I had fallen over at school. Why did I do this? The answer is simple. I loved Mum and Dad and didn't want them to die. My Grandmother threatened me each day saying that if I told what was going on, she would kill my parents. She repeatedly promised she would make sure Mum and

Dad died that very day. Those sadistic threats were more than enough to keep my mouth permanently shut. At this time I was about six years old and young enough to believe all I was told. Although my Father didn't see or hear the actual cruelty first hand, one questions to this day the degree to which my Grandmother's overall intimidation keep Dad from ever doing anything?

As time passed my parents couldn't stand my Grandmother any longer and in a desperate attempt to escape her, they sold their house and moved to the other side of Southend. The move did little good because a month later they looked out of the window to see a removal van being unloaded with familiar furniture. Gran had bought the bungalow opposite.

From my earliest memories, Gran was around our house every day, running the show and her moving in opposite meant nothing was ever going to change.

I'm told I was a delightful baby - happy, easy to please, contented and fun. I was a bright child and surprised my parents when I started walking and talking at a very early age. However, around the age of three I began to suffer from many stress-related illnesses such as asthma and hay fever. In essence I became a disturbed child.

As early as I can remember my Mother suffered from bad migraine attacks. The attacks were bad enough but there was something else - Mum regularly consumed vast quantities of tranquillisers. If it wasn't the migraines, she was often spaced out and fast asleep on heavy doses of tranquillisers. Frequently Mum was laid up in bed for days at a time, leaving me to practically run the house.

From the age of seven it was often left to me to prepare
and cook the family evening meal, which had to be ready
and waiting as Dad arrived home from work. Sometimes
when he got home Dad would manage to wake Mum and
they would eat their dinner together in the bedroom. Dad
did help a bit but most times he was nursing Mum, and
the washing up was left entirely to me.

During the day when Mum was ill, needing peace and
quiet, she would regularly ask me to phone Gran to stop
her visiting.
"Mum's ill but it's not necessary for you to come round",
I would nervously say but always got the same reply.
"Kay's my daughter – what do you know about looking
after her? You're just an incapable child. I'm coming
round now", my Grandmother would rage.
Feeling a total failure, once again letting Mum down, I'd
return to Mum's bedroom sheepishly explaining that
Gran was on her way. I felt my body tightening up
because for me those days with my Mother in bed and
Gran in charge were the worst. My Grandmother
constantly cleaned and hoovered around Mum, talking to
her without pausing when all my Mother wanted was
peace and quiet.

To escape, Mum always swallowed more tranquillisers to
get off to sleep. This left Gran free to take me to her
bungalow where I would sleep overnight. I had no
choice. With my Mother on drugs and my Father unable
to cope, I had to stay with my Grandmother most
weekends and often during the week. I pleaded with my
Mother not to send me to Gran's but at an early age, I
was programmed to go. My Mother would say:
"For my sake please go".

I knew if I didn't, Gran would be nasty to my Mum and even as a seven-year-old child, I wanted to keep the peace.

I felt it very unfair that my older brother was always allowed to stay with Mum even if Dad wasn't back from work yet.

It was in my Grandmother's bungalow during those horrific visits that my Anorexia nervosa began.

I was five years old.

Meal times with Gran were tortuous experiences. Every meal was either fish with lots of bones or fatty meat and piles of mashed potatoes. If I tried to take the bones out from the fish Gran always shouted at me:
"Don't pick at it like a little fusspot. Just eat it."
Then she'd scoop up forkfuls of the fish and shove it in my mouth. If I didn't swallow immediately she would hit me hard on the leg shouting:
"Swallow it! Swallow it!"
Petrified I obeyed, often choking on the bones. After I had finished every last scrap of food Gran would say:
"Now are you satisfied you fat pig? Wash up you fat little horror."
I felt so alone washing up those dishes. To escape my Grandmother, I often locked myself in the toilet but as soon as she realised where I was, she banged angrily on the door.

At my Grandmother's, bath times were horrible. I could feel her hands washing me all over my body as she said:

"You are fat and fat children grow up to be fat adults."
Standing naked in front of the mirror drying myself after
each bath, she would say:
"Look at your fat legs!"

Confused, later back at home I always asked my Mum
and Dad:
"Do I have fat legs?"
"Of course not" was their reply, with a puzzled look at
such a strange question. Why they never asked that
seven-year-old where her fear of fat legs came from is
questionable to say the least.

My Grandmother made a point of honing in on my
weaknesses, one of which was being afraid of the dark. In
her house I was made to sleep in a pitch-black room with
the windows blacked out like in wartime.
"Its safer in the pitch dark", she would say. "When the
monsters come in at least they can't see you".
At that time I was about eight years old and terrified.
Sometimes I crept out of bed and opened the door so I
could see a minute crack of light but inevitably, on one of
her patrols, she'd scream:
"Don't be pathetic! Children your age aren't scared like
you"
The door would close tight, leaving me alone in the dark.

In the mornings when I woke, Gran was in the kitchen,
cooking a huge breakfast with slices of toast so thick I
had to push them into my mouth. I always ate everything
for fear of another harsh smack. At the end of every visit,
Gran would say to me:
"Tell your parents anything and your Mum and Dad will
be dead today."

Picturing my parents dead in their coffins, I never said a word. Sometimes on my overnight stays, Mum would send children's books with me to Gran's. My Grandmother would read me these stories but make Sleeping Beauty wonderfully thin or Cinderella skinny as a rake.

Those stays with Gran, which I called "Horrible Fat Days", are etched in my memory. It's very painful to look back, remembering her words:
"You are just fat and useless!"
As much as I wanted to, I couldn't tell a living soul what was going on. I loved Mum and Dad and didn't want them dead. But there was another reason, which got stronger as I got older and didn't believe any more that Gran would actually murder my parents. This other cruel and vicious reason led me to become anorexic. My Grandmother had by now convinced me that my parents didn't love me because I was fat.

I became more and more frightened that if I asked Mum and Dad if I was fat, they would say:
"Yes Anna, Gran's not lying - you really are fat but we just didn't want to tell you."

The torment wasn't only at home with my Grandmother, we also had horrific trips out. Gran had a twisted mind. One of her favourite tricks was to ask me if I wanted a present, show me the present in the shop window, even let me hold it and then take it away, telling me I didn't deserve the gift. For a young child, this was torture. Another horrible trick of hers was to say she was going to take me to a swimming pool but once there, instead of letting me join in and go swimming would make me just sit and watch the other swimmers enjoying themselves.

I was six years old when Gran took me and my cousin Tom to London to see the Christmas displays at Hamleys toyshop. I had been looking forward to this trip for a whole week. On the train into London, my Grandmother kept repeating to me that I must never leave her side once we got to Hamleys. She kept on so much that when we arrived I stuck to her like glue, petrified I would get lost.

When we arrived at this famous toy store we went first to the cuddly animal display on the fourth floor. I couldn't believe my eyes. There were so many beautiful stuffed animals! I pointed out to Gran the most adorable toy dog that I'd ever seen but she merely sneered, telling me I'd never get a dog like that because an awful child like me didn't deserve to have one. I looked back at the display with tears in my eyes and stood there for a few moments.

When I turned round, my Grandmother had vanished.

I was alone, lost in that enormous toy store!

Sobbing, I frantically ran around searching for my Grandmother. How had I managed to lose her? I trembled with fear, knowing how angry she would be. Gran did not tolerate any disobedience. Much later, my Grandmother suddenly reappeared and my fears were realised. Grabbing me by the arm she dragged me out of the store, shouting at me what a bad and disobedient girl I was. Tears streamed down my face. I felt so humiliated. The trip I had so much looked forward to had ended in disaster and Gran made me believe it was entirely my fault.

Not until many years later did I realise that my Grandmother had deliberately planned to lose me in that store. She had engineered this whole episode. Any other grandparent who loses a child, immediately puts out an urgent message on the shop's public address system. I was left for ages – alone, bewildered and abandoned. This wasn't the only time. There were numerous occasions when my Grandmother would slyly abandon me at railway stations and shopping centres to always return like a heroine rescuing me, when I was crying my eyes out.

On another visit to London, Gran took my younger cousin Tom and I to Madame Tussauds. She took us straight to the Chamber of Horrors.
"Are we all going in Granny?" I asked, feeling quite nervous.
I thought, if I went in holding her hand, maybe I wouldn't feel too frightened. My Grandmother turned to me and coldly told me that Tom was too young and such a terrifying exhibit would give him nightmares. She insisted I went in alone. Pushing me in, she whispered in my ear that I belonged in these rooms, with all the other people with disfigured and mutilated faces. I was an extremely fat and ugly child and would fit in perfectly in the Horror Chamber. Alone I ran through, past all the monsters, to find Gran waiting outside with her usual grin.

Later, after taking my cousin Tom home, it was back to that bungalow for more fish bones and mountains of mashed potatoes.

Why didn't I say anything?

Was I scared of my Grandmother with her murderous threats?

Or was I afraid to hear my parents say:
"No we don't love you - you are fat"?

As a ten-year-old, if I said nothing I was safe but if I confronted Mum and Dad, perhaps I was frightened I would lose them altogether. This became the pattern of my life.

Be a doormat and be accepted.

Be a doormat and be loved.

Be a thin doormat and be loved even more.

Years later on the verge of death fighting Anorexia nervosa in intensive care, I could still see those plates piled high with food.

ME AGED 6

ME AGED 9 MARK AGED 11

ME AGED 2 WITH MARK AND DAD

ME AGED 6 ON A HOLIDAY BOAT
WITH MARK AND MUM

Chapter 2

AGED 11 TO 13

In 1979, I took the 11+ exam trying to qualify for the town's grammar school Westcliff High, an all girls school. Westcliff was the top local school. It had 800 girls with everyone wearing identical navy uniforms. For years, my Grandmother had always tried to convince me I was stupid and as usual I was petrified I would fail. It was perhaps the fear of my Grandmother's ridicule that spurred me on to pass, and pass I did.

When the results came through, Gran could hardly hide her disappointment. I'd passed the exam with the highest ever score of 98%. I now moved from the school opposite our home to Westcliff High three miles away. It was ironic because Gran herself had just left my new school, where she had worked as a secretary for the last twenty years.

Recently I found out the bizarre medical history of two of her close colleagues who worked in the same office. One developed anorexia at the age of fifty-five, for the first time ever. Another colleague became very depressed. I wonder how many other people who crossed my Grandmother's path became disturbed.

For me, as an eleven-year-old, starting the new school was the light at the end of a long dark tunnel. This was the first taste of freedom from my Grandmother that I'd ever experienced. Until then, at Junior school, I had gone home for lunch each day to find Gran always waiting around our house, ready to deal out a fresh round of scorn as soon as she had me alone. On the odd occasion she wasn't there, I knew for sure she would be back when I came home in the afternoon, to dish out another daily diet of torment.

Going to the new school entailed a three-mile bike ride each day. Leaving at 8.00 every morning, I would not arrive back until 4.30 in the afternoon, even later if I joined one of the many after-school activities. Now I had a significant period of time away from Gran, I felt a tremendous relief. As I walked out the house in the morning I knew that at least for a few hours I would be free. Cycling home each evening I prayed:
"Please God don't let Gran be in tonight."
My Grandmother's abuse had by now become a living nightmare, a real life horror movie waiting for me in my own home.

After regular lessons I joined every possible after-school group, just so that I could stay later in the evenings and not have to go home. Hockey, Computer Studies and Music - anything to prevent me from having to see my Grandmother. My parents, unaware of my misery, didn't realise the true reason I joined so many extra groups; they just thought I was a high achiever.

When there were no additional activities, I went swimming instead, for sessions lasting up to four hours. In the water I was free of Gran. The pool gave me warmth and security - no one could hurt me in that womb like environment. I got medals for my swimming but, thinking my parents wouldn't be particularly interested in them, I just put them away on top of my wardrobe.

I was escaping my Grandmother but the price was high. To avoid her, I was pushing myself physically and mentally to the absolute max, studying until the early hours of each morning. Always scared of Gran's reaction to my school results, I felt a total failure whenever I received B grades instead of A's.

Around this time the verbal abuse from my Grandmother went into overdrive. That old woman appeared to me like a dragon breathing fire. There were many bad times but one remains in my mind above all the others. One day I came home to find my entire collection of china animals with their heads broken off. Only the guinea pig, who was very fat, lay in the middle intact. As usual, too intimidated to tell my parents, I hid the pieces on top of my wardrobe.

When we were younger, my brother Mark and I often played together but now he was sixteen years old and had become more distant. It was like he wasn't even in the house. He just stayed in his room studying his collection of tropical fish. For hours he stared at the fish with his nose pressed up against the tank. Dad spent a lot of time looking after Mum who was more and more frequently ill in bed but even when my Father wasn't doing that, with so many other interests, Dad was hardly ever available for me. Model aircraft and butterfly collecting were just two of the hobbies that somehow denied me the love and affection I so desperately needed.

Love. Attention. I didn't get it.

Alone physically and emotionally as I grew up, I became more vulnerable to my Grandmother's tirades. I tried so desperately to escape but the route I was taking was the highway to Anorexia nervosa.

Day by day, year by year, trying to escape the anguish inflicted by Gran, I continued to force myself to go on at a level mentally and physically beyond my limits.

The inevitable had to happen and it did.

I was thirteen when, just into my third year at Westcliff, I collapsed.

In the music class I was playing a solo when suddenly I dropped my tenor recorder and fell in a heap on the floor. In front of the entire class I was violently sick and cried. The head teacher drove me home. My Mother put me to bed and there I stayed. For the next three months I was totally unable to move, never getting out of bed. Just lying there all day every day, I was practically paralysed. Our GP, Dr Chambers, initially diagnosed me with some form of a debilitating virus but remained unsure as to whether or not it was glandular fever. Dr Chambers was well known to me. He had been our family doctor since I could remember and had frequently visited my Mum. In fact it was Dr Chambers that Mum would always ring for her private prescriptions for more tranquillisers.

During those three months in bed I was to become the perfect victim for my Grandmother. It was impossible for Mum to always be with me, since she now had a part time job, teaching at the local infant school, and the rest

of the family to look after. I would have been very happy
just left on my own but Gran however had other plans.
Mum left for work every day at 9.00 am and within
seconds, I could hear a front door key turning. It was my
Grandmother arriving. She stayed each day until 3.30 pm
and for the majority of that time, sat in a rocking chair
opposite my bed. All day she kept on at me, constantly
nagging. If a fat person appeared on TV she would
comment they were grotesque like me. I'll never know
how my parents really viewed her coming round each
day. Surely they could not still believe she was a caring
Grandmother? For whatever reason, she had her own key
to the front door and the visits continued. Gran held me
prisoner, I was a totally captive audience and she made
the most of it. Each morning she reminded me that I was
getting further and further behind with my schoolwork by
staying in bed.

Hovering round me for hours, she filled my head with her
poisonous messages, telling me I was a lazy, horrible
child who just pretended to be ill and only ever caused
problems for everybody.

My Grandmother's indoctrination confused me, making
me think perhaps I was pretending to be ill. Afraid I
might be faking, I began to force myself to sit upright in
bed, an immense struggle because my body had given up.
Each night I would wait until my parents were downstairs
and then grip hold of the side of the bed and stand upright
for as long as physically possible. I timed myself, each
night managing slightly longer every time.

As the weeks grew into months, my Doctor started to
become very concerned and began to visit every day. He

explained to Mum that although any virus would now have passed, he was very concerned about me because I was losing all my muscle tone. Though he couldn't find anything physically wrong with me, I was obviously extremely ill.

The doctor began to suspect I might have clinical depression. Totally unaware of the constant verbal abuse I was receiving, he felt that the virus could have triggered the depression and started me on a course of mild anti-depressants. Should a doctor give a 13-year old child anti-depressants?

A short while later, getting concerned about the lack of response to the medication, he referred me to a specialist from the local hospital. A lady consultant specialising in women's medical problems visited our house. After a thorough and brusque examination, she stated quite bluntly that she could find absolutely nothing physically wrong with me. She was however very puzzled about why I had a covering of soft downy hair all over my body.

One of the classic symptoms of Anorexia nervosa is the appearance of fine facial and body hair (lanugo). This downy hair appears on the sufferer's body in an attempt to somehow keep that person warm. As a person loses weight, they lose their fat reserves and the body starts to freeze. Surely a qualified consultant should have known what this symptom could indicate. My body had now begun to shut down physically.

This was the onset of my Anorexia nervosa.

The consultant was very unfriendly and upon leaving our house, she commented to my Mum and Dad that there was absolutely nothing wrong with me. It was all in my mind and I should be sent back to school immediately.

That night my Grandmother appeared at my bedroom door with a triumphant grin. The consultant had proved her to be right. With venom in her voice, she started on me again, repeating what an extremely difficult child I was, faking this illness just to get more attention.

Over that Christmas period I desperately tried to make myself well, forcing myself to go downstairs and pretending I was feeling much better than I really was. I continually felt very weak but never let on.

The consultant sent a report to Dr Chambers saying I should go back to school immediately but our local doctor disagreed and stood his ground. It was plainly obvious to him that I was far from well and unable to return to school. Early in January 1982, Dr Chambers suggested psychiatry for the first time.
"I'm still very concerned about you Anna. You look so pale and thin. I suspect there is a psychological side to your illness and I really think you should see a psychiatrist."

A week or so later I started to see the first of many psychiatrists in my life. Dr Henry, an Austrian, was a tall man in his late fifties. He always carried an old battered briefcase, which he laid on the bed next to me. As a consultant he usually treated adults but I was 13 years old and he was really at a loss as to whether to class me as an adult or a child. The first time I saw him, my Mum was in the room with me so I couldn't talk freely and became very defensive, hardly answering any of his probing questions. It made no real difference because even if Mum hadn't been there, I was still far too afraid of the retaliation from my Grandmother to begin telling the truth.

Instead I deliberately misled the doctor to draw him away from the true situation at home, leaving my Grandmother completely out of the picture. This left Dr Henry thinking my problems were bullying or something else at school.

Convinced I was acutely depressed, he started me on another type of anti-depressant. However nothing worked and when I next saw him, four weeks later, there were no signs of improvement, so once again he switched brands. When this latest brand failed, Dr Henry continued to stab in the dark trying new drugs on me. The dosages increased until, at the tender age of thirteen, I was now taking adult levels of anti-depressant tablets. My system soon started to react adversely to those pills, causing me to hallucinate. I saw black cats jumping out of walls, faces of the devil laughing at me on the wallpaper and every time I closed my eyes, more frightening images surfaced. I was too scared to go to sleep, afraid bad nightmares would begin and would sit up all night crying.

The doctor's answer to my insomnia was typical – more drugs, heavy barbiturates!

These potent sleeping pills knocked me out but still the horrific nightmares began. These were not normal nightmares, however. I would have eight or nine frightening short dreams, one after another. All the nightmares concerned various people but always there was a recurring theme. In each dream people were mutilated, with their limbs being hacked off. One morning at 2.00 am, I stumbled into my parents' bedroom, drugged and dazed, crying for help. My Mum was on one of her heavy tranquilliser nights and couldn't wake up. Dad had to take me back to my bed and slept on the floor beside me, vowing they would put a stop to all the medications.

The following morning Dad phoned the hospital, only to discover Dr Henry had flown out to New Zealand. He now frantically explained to the doctor on duty about the effect the anti-depressants were having on their thirteen-year-old daughter but was told that the registrar had absolutely no authority to change my medication. For the next 24 hours, my parents reluctantly followed the hospital's instructions. It all got much worse and with me still hallucinating, Mum and Dad were forced to take matters into their own hands. They stopped all the drugs. As soon as they did, the hallucinations started to fade and, unable to keep my eyes open, later that afternoon I fell into a semi-coma. Suddenly the nightmares re-exploded with a vengeance and I was convulsing with the most ghoulish nightmares of my entire life.

I still vividly remember that afternoon and always will. Mum was sitting beside me in the chair, hugging me as I cried and screamed. I tried to keep awake but just couldn't stop myself from falling asleep, each time re-awaking within minutes, screaming. For two hours my parents alternated, one holding me whilst the other desperately tried to find a doctor.

The whole episode was caused by a violent reaction to the strong drugs and the hallucinatory nightmares were symptoms of withdrawal.

Over the next week my parents tried everything to pull me round. They even bought me a new kitten to cheer me up but at this stage I was so desperately ill, all I could do was watch the little black and white kitten stumble about. As each day passed I became more and more withdrawn.

I was due to see Dr Henry immediately he returned from New Zealand but by now our local GP was very concerned and visited our house twice a day. Extremely worried and not knowing what to do himself, he called in a paediatrician who immediately admitted me to Southend General Hospital.

Chapter 3

PSYCHIATRIC TREATMENT AT THIRTEEN

"I don't want to go", I cried.

For about an hour I kicked up such a fuss, refusing to get out of the bed and be taken to hospital.

"Leave me alone", I shouted, holding onto the bedcovers.

My protests meant nothing because I was so weak and the paediatrician and my parents had little difficulty in carrying me to my Father's car.

Anorexia nervosa now held me firmly in its clutches.

Mum and Dad drove me to the local hospital where, upon arrival, I was put in a wheelchair and taken to the children's ward. I was definitely too old for the children's ward but the doctors were unhappy to have me in the adult women's ward, where gynaecological and other "grown up" problems were constantly discussed.

Mum and Dad stayed with me for a while but when they were about to leave, I began crying.
"Don't leave me. Take me home."
It was all very upsetting, with the nurses practically holding me down as my parents walked away.

I was very mixed up, not really aware of what was going on. While other young teenage girls my age were out chasing boys here I was, an emotional and physical cripple in hospital and nobody, including the doctors, really knew why. Unable to sleep on the first night, I cried until morning.

The following day I was seen by a constant stream of consultants, registrars, housemen and nurses. They all asked me dozens of complicated questions. On top of this, numerous tests were carried out including an ECG. An ECG measures the heartbeat, testing for irregularities. I was thirteen years old and felt like a freak with all the wires attached to me.

This was the spring of 1982 and over the next month in hospital I lost weight rapidly. I just couldn't eat any of the food. My stomach wouldn't tolerate anything and I now felt as though there was this huge solid mass of pain inside me and there really was no space for food.

The children's ward, a detached annex, was designed for little kids only and I was forced to take my meals with toddlers, sitting on low tiny chairs around a circular table. Crouched down with those little boys and girls I felt so humiliated and out of place. I didn't belong here, being treated like an infant, when at home for years I'd been trying to behave like an adult. Every time the nurses looked over, I pretended to chew food but later I'd spit into a tissue and as soon as no one was looking, I would throw it away.

In the children's ward there was a girl with water on the brain. She had an abnormally large head and had been totally abandoned by her parents and left for the hospital to bring up. This girl had now been in hospital for four years and looked like staying there forever. My Grandmother always said I was the same as this girl, disfigured and ugly and it wouldn't be long before my parents abandoned me, just like her. At 13 years old, I still believed my Gran and a part of me thought this would all come true.

The first couple of weeks in that hospital were the worst. I didn't know anyone and strange doctors kept appearing and reappearing with new questions. Every day there were more and more frightening tests.

Mum and Dad tried to be with me as much as possible but of course their work meant that they were frequently unavailable. Gran as usual took over, arriving each day at 2.00pm and staying until 5.00pm when most days thankfully my Mother arrived. Exactly what my Mother thought of Gran's visits I'll never know. Did Mum actually want my Grandmother to come and see me each day or was she just too afraid to stop her?

Gran, determined to continue with her constant brainwashing, was also herself desperately afraid that I might start talking to a nurse or doctor about the way she'd always treated me. She sat on my bed whispering her threats. In no uncertain terms she told me that if I ever told a single soul about anything that had occurred, the punishment would be unbearable.

She kept telling me my parents would die soon anyway and then she would bring me up alone. What did I believe? Would my Grandmother actually kill my parents or not? Really the psychological damage had already been done eight years before to me then, a petrified 5-

year-old locked up in her Grandmother's bungalow. Now I was a young teenager believing every word Gran ever spoke. I was terrified and stayed silent when questioned about my home life. I was convinced that no doctor would ever believe a word of my story anyway. Gran often spoke to the staff so charmingly and I was sure they firmly believed she was just a very sweet and caring Grandmother.

The doctors and nurses continued to be extremely puzzled about my condition. I'd entered hospital a very ill child, but even under their care I was showing no signs of improvement. In fact the opposite was happening. Rather than making progress, I was actually deteriorating. My weight had started to drop dramatically and the pair of dungarees that had fitted quite snugly when I was admitted, now hung loosely.

While I was in hospital, I was befriended by a Staff Nurse called Nicki, who was extremely caring and took a special interest in me. Through her intervention I didn't have to eat meals at the table with the little children any more. She took it on herself to order special menus for me of healthier foods, fruit and salads. Additionally I was given a fortified food supplement in an attempt to help me regain some strength. Nicki began taking me out for the afternoon for car rides to her flat, trying all the time to get me to talk openly with her. She knew something was wrong with my home life but just couldn't get me to open up and divulge what it was. Even though I trusted Nicki, I found it impossible to tell her anything because my Grandmother's fearsome threats were far too powerful.

After I'd been in the hospital for about three weeks Dr Henry returned from New Zealand. He arrived on the ward one morning and I was ushered into his office for another lengthy interview. Horrified at the amount of weight I'd lost, he again tried me on yet another different type of anti-depressant. Once more I was given a very strong adult dose, even though I was only a child. Within a few days I started to suffer from the usual side effects. The hallucinations returned, but this time something even more frightening happened.

I noticed it after a teacher from my school called round on a visit, bringing me some books so that I could try and catch up with the lessons. After she left I picked up one of the books and tried to start work but the words swam before my eyes. I couldn't make any sense of the writing. Everything was scrambled. All I could see were meaningless sentences. Terrified, I called a nurse and tried to make her understand what was happening, but no one seemed to believe me. I was very distressed when that evening my parents were told that I was being extremely belligerent, pretending there was something wrong with my vision just to avoid the schoolwork.

Dad found it all very strange. I'd always been a conscientious child who never needed reminding about homework. My grades had always been high. I tried to explain to Dad what was happening to the words on the page and how bewildered I felt. Thankfully Dad believed me. Having seen me experience the hallucinations only a month before he didn't doubt me and furiously asked the registrar on duty to stop my medications. My parents were very annoyed when they were once again told that only a consultant was able to change a patient's medication and Dr Henry would not be back in the hospital for another four days.

"Four days", my Mother screamed.

It was at this point that my parents' patience finally snapped. They had allowed their daughter to be admitted to hospital several weeks previously with the promise that she'd be returned to them well and healthy. Now she was even sicker than ever. Her weight had dropped dramatically, she had no colour left in her face and in a totally drugged state she couldn't even read any more.

My Mum had always been an extremely mild mannered lady, but that day all her restraint disappeared. She went crazy, shouting at the senior houseman on duty. Mum was adamant and insisted he stopped the medicines that were continually being pumped into me.

There was panic round the hospital with everybody arguing. My parents wouldn't give up and eventually the senior houseman located another consultant. The medication was stopped but the damage however had already been done. The drugs, this time, had a lasting effect on my brain. The hallucinations didn't fade and proper visual perception never returned. The monsters, here to stay, had taken up residence inside my head permanently.

It was around this time, I think the hospital started to suspect that I was being abused. Unfortunately the doctors were completely misled by my Grandmother's charm and my silence led them to think it was Mum who was treating me badly. Unable to discover the truth, the doctors decided to restrict my parents' visits.

Mum and Dad coming to see me each day, had been my only glimpse of light and in restricting their visits my condition deteriorated further. I am sure my Grandmother all along gently drip-fed the doctors the idea that my Mother was abusing me. By pushing the blame onto my parents it deflected all suspicion away from herself.

A week or so later Dr Henry once more visited me on the ward. Gran was there at the time. The doctor seemed totally unsure of what course of action to take next. Having tried every conceivable type of test available, I think he was giving up. After talking with me, my Grandmother was called to Dr Henry's office and they spoke together alone for quite a while. Gran returned to my bedside with her eyes gleaming. Standing over me she announced triumphantly,
"You are coming home with me."
This was strange, to say the least. Why weren't my parents consulted regarding my discharge? It was all so unbelievable and years later, I actually found out, my parents considered suing the hospital. I was very excited at the idea of going home to my parents and wanted to go down to the payphone to ring Mum but Gran refused.

"Your parents are far too busy to come and collect you and besides, they don't want you home anyway. Why do you think you're in hospital?" Gran asked. "I'll tell you why", she continued. "Because your Mum and Dad can't cope with you. If it wasn't for me, you wouldn't be going home at all", Gran continued.

"But I can't come home with you - I haven't got my suitcase", I pleaded.

"You don't need a suitcase", she said, handing me a black plastic bin liner. "Just put all your rubbish in there, we're going right now."

And so the two of us left - me with my black bag over my shoulder, looking like a gypsy.

To my surprise, my Grandmother took me to my parents' house. We were alone for a couple of hours and the verbal abuse continued. That evening, when Mum and Dad arrived home, they couldn't believe their eyes to see me sitting on my bed next to the black plastic bin bag.

Amazingly Mum now took some time off work and having her around was good for me. For once I seemed to be getting the attention I so badly needed. My Mother was making a special effort in caring for me, cooking meals to tempt my delicate appetite. While Mum remained at home I started to gain a little weight and became stronger.

I stayed indoors most of the time, pottering round the house, building up my strength. My Mother was out one day, when in her bedroom I found one of her infant school teaching books. Suddenly I realised I could actually read the cover which had just one word written on it. Excitedly I turned to the first page and found two words, which I could also read. By the time I reached the fourth page however, there was a whole sentence of about six words and in my head they jumbled incomprehensibly. I went back a page and once again read those three words 'Janet and John' correctly.

My problem seemed to arise when there were more than three or four words together. In my bedroom I found a piece of card and cut out a section in the middle like a miniature picture frame. All I could see through the hole in this card were the three words that I placed the card over. This worked. Every time I placed the card on three new words I could read them. I decided to try this on one of my own books. Obviously the hole in the card had to be decreased in size, as the print on the page of an adult's book was much smaller, but the principle was the same and it worked. It was difficult to use this card but I was able to read once more, even if it was slowly.

As the weeks passed, I got stronger and so desperately wanted to be normal, to read again and be back at school. But I was so confused.

Why was this happening to me?

What was the meaning of it all?

Would I ever get better?

In May 1982 I had my first out patients appointment to see Dr Henry at Rochford Hospital. This turned out to be yet another intimidating afternoon. The waiting room was full of severely mentally ill patients and to a very nervous 13-year-old this was very scary. One woman was screaming and refused to get out of her chair and it took four nurses to shift her. Another man with a bad leg kept hopping round the room talking to himself. As always, I found Dr Henry very difficult to talk to regarding my home life. After our meeting he sent a report to Dr

Chambers stating that, regardless of my claim of reading complications, I should return to school immediately.

A day or so later when I was told about the doctors report I became very frightened. Although I genuinely wanted to go back to school, the very idea of being back in the classroom filled me with panic. I hadn't been there for seven months and was now terribly behind in the lessons. I still couldn't read or write more than three words at a time. How was I going to learn with the words all merging together on a blackboard? What would the other pupils say? Would they all make fun of me? All the other girls at school would ask where had I been.

So many questions raced round my head.

The following Monday morning my parents drove me back to school. Mum and I went in together to see the Headmistress. My Mother spent a long time explaining to Miss Howard all the problems I was going through. Mum had with her a letter from the doctor, which explained the medical reasons why I'd been absent from school. The Headmistress listened carefully and after reading the letter from Dr Chambers, spoke to me for a long time. She was extremely understanding and thought it a good idea if I was to be allowed to return to my old class and just sit in, listening to all that was happening. I wouldn't have to participate in the lessons in any way but by being there, I'd feel included and perhaps pick up some knowledge.

On my first day back at school, I was extremely relieved to find all of my teachers very sympathetic. They included me in their classes as best they could but also made sure that they didn't put me under any pressure. My Maths and English teachers were especially considerate and helpful in making the remaining time to the end of the third year bearable.

In June we had our usual end of year exams. As I had missed so much work and still couldn't read or write competently, the Headmistress decided I should be allowed to take the tests at home with the help of my parents. Mum and Dad would read the questions to me and write my answers in the spaces provided. The school, of course, didn't expect me to do brilliantly but wanted to know my level of knowledge and whether or not I should re-sit the third year. When the results came in I was called into Miss Howard's office. She was very pleasantly surprised with the results of the mock examinations I'd done at home and said I could choose to stay back and re-do the third year or move onto the fourth with all my friends. I opted to move on, even though it was probably going to be quite a struggle to make up a whole year's work.

Chapter 4

MUM'S LEAVING ON A JET PLANE

I was now just 14 years old and for almost all the summer holidays of 1982, I continually practised reading. Gradually I managed to lengthen the space in the card until I could read six words at a time and returned to school in the autumn to start my 'O' Level studies, with a large collection of specially made reading cards. Not only did I read through these cards, I also had to write through them. I couldn't write at all without the cards. If I wrote more than six words, they scrambled before my eyes becoming totally nonsensical to me.

Throughout that hot summer my weight, although now very low, remained steady. Again I started to believe I was fat and ugly. As I got further into puberty, the monster called Anorexia nervosa was just waiting to pounce. Here I was changing from a child to a woman. I'd had periods for two years, my breasts were beginning to form and I was wearing my first training bra. Where other young girls wanted to show off their shapely new bodies, I just wanted to hide my new curves and stay matchstick thin.

During those school holidays my Grandmother became obsessed with an additional mission apart from terrorising me - my great Uncle Reg (Gran's dead husband's uncle) and his will. Reg wasn't actually dead yet but Gran believed in forward planning.

Gran, who had her eyes on Reg's bungalow and his money, demanded that her son Ron, Mum's younger brother, become executor. Referring to his demands at work, Ron refused. He worked as an Economic Planning Manager for the National Freight Corporation which was an extremely high powered job and he did it very well. However my Grandmother had, over the years, undermined his confidence by constantly commenting on how important it was to look after the job. As a result Ron had become paranoid about losing the position. Having been under considerable pressure from his Mother all his life, by the time Ron was 36 he was taking large numbers of tranquillisers and anti-depressants. Around this time Ron was offered a new position in Cambridgeshire. He saw this as a perfect way of putting some distance between himself and his mother and took the new job.

My Grandmother now turned on Mum to persuade Dad to become the executor. Mum, as usual, afraid to stand up to Gran, reluctantly persuaded Dad to go and see Reg. When they met, Dad had great difficulty communicating with the old man because by this time Reg was almost totally deaf. However Reg liked Dad and gratefully accepted his help.

In December 1983 Uncle Reg finally died and that's when the trouble really started. When the will was read Gran's face dropped, as it became obvious that the old man had changed it dramatically. Gran wasn't left the bungalow she wanted so much. Reg's estate was now to be divided into six equal parts. One sixth going to my Gran, another to my Dad and the final four sixths to separate charities. Gran was absolutely furious. Her plan had failed. Ron was even more annoyed. He'd been left absolutely nothing.

Triggered by her financial loss my Grandmother's maliciousness went into overdrive. She started insulting Mum all the time, putting her down without reprieve. I felt so helpless listening to the constant phone calls of abuse and desperately wanted to grab the receiver and shout at Gran to leave my mother alone. I was nearly 15 years old now but, with so little self-confidence, was unable to stand up to my Grandmother, of all people.

Before long the pressure began to take its toll on my Mother. It did so in the shape of the American pop star John Denver. For most of my childhood I was brought up listening to John Denver songs. My Mother loved his music and Dad would buy her each new record. By the time I was eight I knew every song he'd written off by heart. Mum joined his fan club and soon after went to a live concert at the Royal Albert Hall. After her big night out, thrilled to bits, Mum wrote to him sending a donation of £10 to his charity organisation. A few weeks later, she received a reply signed by John Denver, personally thanking her for her gift of money. Dad framed it and it was hung on the wall in our lounge. During this period, each time Mum returned home from yet another upsetting session with my Grandmother, she used John Denver records as an escape, hiding in a world of her own. Before long John Denver and his music became the most important aspect of her life.

My illness was to become anorexia, my Mum's illness was already John Denver.

At this time Mum was working four mornings a week at
the local Junior School as a supply teacher. Just before
the end of the school term she wrote another letter to
John Denver, this time pretending to be one of her pupils.
Writing as Mary Smith (who was supposed to be a pupil)
she said how much they liked having Mrs Paterson
(herself) as their teacher, and would John Denver please
send her a signed photo, as a thank you from them (the
pupils) since she liked his music so much? Mum's plan
worked and she received another warm reply,
commenting on how much the children she taught
obviously liked her. A signed photo of John Denver was
enclosed. This letter and photograph were promptly
framed and joined the other John Denver picture on the
wall.

By August, Mum was now completely living in her own
fantasy world and had lost all touch with reality. It was
during our summer holiday to Cornwall that year she
asked my Dad if she could send a postcard to John
Denver. He thought it very peculiar but if it made Mum
happy then it was all right with him.

John Denver? Postcards? It was all very worrying.
Mum's bizarre behaviour was exactly what Gran had
predicted. My Grandmother had foreseen this, and told
me repeatedly for years, that because I was such a bad
girl Mum would go mad. Now it was all coming true.
Through the power of Gran's wicked indoctrination I
firmly believed I was to blame and had to be punished.

Mum's behaviour however had one good point - it took
the spotlight off my developing eating disorder and I

could lose more weight easily, without any questions being asked.

In September 1984 the money from Uncle Reg's will was finally distributed, with Dad and Gran both receiving £6000 each. Dad, now fed up with my Grandmother's nagging, worked out that if he and Gran now gave Ron £2000 it would leave them all with an equal share of £4000. Ron, who was at that time extremely depressed, accepted the money without comment. The redistribution of the money didn't really help as Dad had hoped. My Grandmother was still angry and felt extremely hard done by.

As my Grandmother's behaviour worsened, so did my Mum's mental state and my weight dropped accordingly.

It was around that time Mum first began to write for hours on end. One day when she was out, I found pages and pages of strange and bizarre poetry all connected with John Denver the singer. For me, a sixteen-year-old, having my Mum write John Denver poems all day made life even more confusing. From being a very open person, Mum suddenly changed and became extremely secretive. Whenever I found her writing, she would quickly hide the pad.

I didn't understand what was happening to my Mum and I couldn't help her. The person I'd known from childhood had vanished. She didn't want me around and wouldn't confide in me.

On top of her usual tranquillisers, Mum now began taking a very powerful migraine tablet that disturbed her sleep. She was also taking a huge amount of over the counter medications.

With her own home-made cocktail of pills, Mum was now on the verge of madness.

For hours on end Mum wrote constantly to John Denver, sending him letters, photographs and poetry every day. Many years after, we found out she was spending hundreds of pounds on postage and developing costs. Each night she waited until my Father was asleep and then crept out of their bed and went down into the kitchen. She confessed later that she was, at that stage, already planning to leave her family to live with John Denver in the States. My Grandmother in her twisted way, encouraged my Mother, saying her poetry was meaningful and told her,
"Kay, you must keep writing to John Denver. He waits every day for the post to arrive."

I knew at the time something was terribly wrong but never guessed the extent of Mum's sick obsession.

The only way I could cope with it all was to stop eating. I was now disappearing into the world of Anorexia nervosa.

I can still remember the day I made the decision to stop eating. I'd just finished having tea with my family. I went upstairs to listen to some music but didn't even get as far as putting a tape into my machine. Suddenly, there was someone talking in the room. I looked round. There was nobody there but I could clearly hear a voice. Someone was speaking.

"Look at your fat thighs, you pig!"

I looked round the room again but there was nobody there. I looked under the bed. No one. I looked in the wardrobe. No one. I even climbed up and looked on top of the wardrobe but there was no one there. Somebody was still talking, saying:

"Look at your thighs, you big fat pig!"

"There must be someone in the lounge", I thought and ran down the stairs to look.
But there was no one there. I looked everywhere but the whole house was empty. My parents had gone for a walk.
"What's going on? What's going on?" I said to myself.
How can someone be talking to me if there is no one in the house?
"Shut up! Shut up!" I cried but the voice continued.

"Fat thighs! Fat thighs! Fat thighs!"

It was several days before I realised that this voice, which sounded like a person standing next to me, was inside my head. The voice I heard was an authoritative figure, telling me I was fat, although in reality I was a very thin girl. The voice had control of my mind and now my distorted vision could only see an incredibly fat girl every time I looked in the mirror. I couldn't see the person speaking to me but someone was there, and I clearly heard every word and every instruction that was meant to destroy me over the next twenty years. This invisible yet audible voice was now my master. After my first experience of hearing this voice in an empty house, the next time I heard it I didn't bother looking under beds or on top of wardrobes any more. I just listened to the voice.

My Grandmother had been right. From a fat child I'd grown into a fat young woman.

If I could lose weight maybe Mum would get better.

If I was thin maybe Mum and Dad would love me.

If I was thin maybe my Grandmother would love me.

If I was thin, maybe…

That night I decided to cut out all cakes, biscuits, chocolate, and crisps at first, not deserving nice things that only good people were allowed to eat. But within days this wasn't enough. Before long I stopped eating potatoes, bread and other staples, existing solely on fruit, vegetables and yoghurt. To get thinner even quicker, I made myself go through a rigorous exercise programme. I worked out a very long and complicated dance routine that I carried out religiously each day.

The anorexic voice was here to stay.

I now had long detailed conversations with the voice who clearly answered every question I raised. It was a strange voice and I couldn't make out whether it was male or female.

The voice now constantly repeated the words Gran had drummed into me for so many years. My Grandmother didn't even need to be there now. I had my own devil –

the voice. For the next twenty years I was to negotiate
with the voice over what I was and wasn't allowed to do.
Over what I was and wasn't allowed to eat. Over what I
was and wasn't allowed to think. Depending on my own
strength at any particular time, I could put up very valid
arguments but the ultimate decision was the voices and
what the voice said I had to do. If the voice said,

"Eat two less potatoes today",

I ate two less potatoes.

School ended and another year's summer holidays began
and without other distractions, the voice in my head
chanted louder. Obeying instructions, I cut down further
and further on food, exercising even more vigorously. It
was surprisingly easy for me to carry out these changes to
my lifestyle without anyone noticing, especially with
Mum in her bedroom all day. Whenever I entered her
room, I heard the sudden rustle of paper and knew
another notepad had been hurriedly hidden under the
bedcovers.

Hundreds of pages to John Denver.

I was totally horrified to find all the poems in Mum's
cupboard. It all worried me, not only was my Mother's
behaviour very strange but, because I shouldn't have
opened her bedroom cupboard in the first place, I
couldn't even tell my Dad this poetry existed.

My older brother, now 18 years old, was finding home
life very difficult and began staying out as much as
possible. Dad was in London at work for 12 hours every

day, leaving me totally unsupervised and so no one noticed I wasn't eating. When it came to the evening meal, which we had together, I would pretend that I'd been constantly nibbling at food all day and really wasn't hungry.

"Could I please be excused?" I would always say.

The atmosphere in the house, at that time, was so difficult that it was a relief to escape to my room, where I could exercise in peace. I often exercised for many hours at a time, into the early hours of the morning when everybody else was fast asleep.

Mum had by now started to turn away from my Father altogether. She still played her music but waited until my Dad was out of the house. It was as if she was saying John Denver was solely hers and nobody else was allowed to listen. My Father became very frustrated and to escape reality, worked in the garden like never before.

We went to Wales for our family holiday that summer and it turned out to be a nightmare. Mum, drugged out of her mind, would just sit on a window-ledge gazing at the river. During this vacation, my parents had their worst ever row. It started when, in a café, my brother Mark kicked me under the table and Dad told him off. Mum just went mad and minutes later, my parents were screaming at each other in front of the passing crowds along Tenby beach.

Mum and Dad seemed to hate each other now. I was convinced it was just a matter of time before they got divorced.

Throughout the holiday I was cutting back on food constantly. I'd excuse myself early from meal times or arrive late, eating as little as possible without arousing suspicion. All I wanted to do was get back to my room where I frantically exercised, burning off the latest calories I'd consumed. I was losing weight quite rapidly but I'd always worn baggy clothes, so it wasn't that noticeable yet.

After the holiday, returning home, my Grandmother took me to one side and told me my parents would soon get divorced and it was all my fault. Deep down she had always wanted them to split up. She never liked my Dad because through him, she had lost complete control over Mum. Gran loved the prospect of a divorce because with Dad out of the picture, Mum would once more be totally under her control.

My parents' fighting upset me a great deal. Everything now seemed to be falling apart and I wished even more to just disappear. I cut down even further on food until all I ate each day was one diet yoghurt.

In September 1985, I returned to school for the start of my second year of 'A' Levels. This year was also to include a secretarial course, which was to later dramatically change my life. By now I was eating nothing at school all day and avoided food at home. In the evenings, I usually found a plate of food left out for me by my Mum. After thanking her I would disappear with it upstairs, saying I had a huge amount of homework to do. It's sad looking back, that no one ever questioned why I was spending so much time in my bedroom. Previously I'd always completed my schoolwork sitting at the kitchen table but now I couldn't do that any more, for obvious reasons.

Mum had a habit of leaving a few biscuits out for me every afternoon. I took them and carefully wrapped each one in a small plastic bag, hiding them in my cupboards. For some weird reason I couldn't waste those biscuits, that would have been more bad behaviour. I just kept them in the vague hope that one day, I'd be a worthy and good enough person, who was allowed to eat them. Like all anorexics, I felt unworthy, not good enough to deserve to eat biscuits but I lived in the vain hope, that one day, even I might become worthwhile enough to eat a biscuit. As a suffering anorexic I always felt the lowest of the low.

I lost more weight but even though I still wore baggy clothes, by this time it became obvious I was very thin. By now I weighed just 7 stones (98 lbs.) and at 5 foot 8 inches, that meant I was extremely underweight. The correct weight for a girl of that height was between 9½ and 10½ stones (133 and 147 lbs.). My teachers at school started to notice the change in me. One afternoon the deputy head kept me behind after a sociology class and said how concerned all the staff were that I seemed to have lost so much weight. Was I eating enough? I needed to build up my strength if I was to pass the final examinations. I really had to start eating properly.
"Go home and have a good dinner", she emphasised.

That weekend my brother Mark, who was away at college, came home for a visit and having not seen me for a while, was shocked at the change in me. He asked Mum if I was becoming anorexic.

For a brief while Mum snapped out of her dream world. Mark's anorexic comment made her think. She hadn't seen me eat a proper meal for ages, or even nibble on crisps and other snacks the way I used to. I was always up in my room and yes, I definitely was losing weight. My jeans hung on me and I was constantly cold, often sitting as close as I possibly could to the fire in the evenings. All this began to arouse my Mother's suspicions. When I was at school one day, Mum went up to my bedroom and started opening drawers, discovering bags and bags of carefully packaged biscuits. Every biscuit I'd ever been given was hidden there. I never thought Mum would ever look through my private possessions and when she did, it felt like a betrayal. Now there was nowhere to hide my food.

When I got home that night I found my Mother surrounded by hundreds of bags of biscuits. Panicking, I started to run but Mum caught up with me at the bottom of the garden. Tears were pouring down both of our faces. She cried and hugging me took me back into the house, saying:
"Come on, I am going to make you an omelette, you won't find that hard to eat."

My immediate feeling was one of tremendous relief. I'd spent the last five months starving myself. My stomach rumbled constantly and the pain was intense. The truth was out and finally someone was allowing me to eat again. I sat down with Mum and we agreed that if I'd start to eat proper meals again then she wouldn't have to tell Dad. It would stay between the two of us. For two days I managed to follow my Mother's plan but then the anorexic guilt soon returned.

The voice took over again and turned up the volume.

"You are not allowed to eat! What was the point in you losing all that weight to become thin if you now just pile it back on again?"

Obeying the voice immediately, I reduced my intake but this time I had to be even more careful. Mum knew about my hiding places. It had to appear as if I was eating. Breakfast was easy, I pretended to eat when Mum was in the bathroom. Lunch was equally simple. I just threw my packed lunch in the bin before I reached school, pretending I'd eaten it earlier in the day. The evening meal was more complicated but I would slip as much as I could into tissues and hankies and carefully dispose of it in the dustbin when no one was looking. I lived in constant fear that someone would find out I was disposing of food. Physically I was by now in constant pain. My stomach hurt, my bones and muscles ached and all the time I was freezing cold. My circulation no longer working, meant my hands and feet were permanently blue.

Ironically it was now, at the real onset of my Anorexia nervosa, that Mum had her own nervous breakdown.

Mum believed it was time to leave her family and live with John Denver in America and secretly she had worked out an elaborate leaving plan. She completed a passport application form and early one afternoon took the train to London, going to the Passport Office. Mum went in person to avoid the risk of the passport being returned through the post, scared Dad might have opened the letter.

A day or so later I came home from school to find my Mother in the garden sitting on a suitcase. Her eyes were glazed as she told me she was leaving that day to live in America with John Denver. I was shocked and ran into the house to phone Dad. Inside Mum's clothes were everywhere, strewn across the floor. In her bedroom her wardrobes were empty.

On the mantlepiece were three letters, one to Dad, one to my brother Mark and one to me.

At first Mum refused to move from the garden but eventually I managed to get her inside and helped her up to her bed. An hour or so later my Father arrived but by now Mum was fast asleep. The three letters were still on the mantlepiece and Dad read his. With tears in his eyes, he told me Mum was leaving him for another man. I'll never forget my Father's face that day. With Dad still crying I opened my letter, which simply said the same.

Dad was in a terrible state and became even more distressed when he opened Mum's suitcase and discovered literally hundreds of tablets. For the first time ever, we both realised the extent of Mum's pill taking.

Now crying hysterically, my Father woke Mum and begged her to stay. Dad somehow persuaded Mum that night to stop her pills and she agreed to cut down considerably, there and then. The days and weeks that followed were very traumatic but Mum did stay and gradually became more like her old self again. As the months passed, to some extent, she returned to normality. She never played John Denver's records again and his name became a taboo subject in our house.

John Denver had gone but my Grandmother, who had systematically reduced Mum to a nervous wreck and steered me into the world of anorexia, was still there, feeling as smug as ever.

Some months later a letter came, offering me an escape from Gran.

I had been accepted at Whitelands College to do a four-year degree course in Biology and Sociology, which meant I was to be a border at the college 60 miles away from my Grandmothers clutches.

Unfortunately for me, it was now too late. I was losing weight all the time.

I was well on my way to full-blown Anorexia nervosa.

ME (CENTRE) AT SCHOOL AGED 17

Chapter 5

STARVING MYSELF AT COLLEGE

In September 1986, aged 18, I lived away from home for
the first time and took up residence at Whitelands
College, Putney. The usual trauma started even before I
left. My Grandmother, as always, decided she wanted to
come to London to settle me into college. For the first
time in my life somehow I actually said no to her. I'll
never know where I found the courage, that day, because
usually I said yes to everything. But, there was no way I
was going to look an idiot. The other students wouldn't
arrive at college with their Grandmothers in tow.

My first few days at college were extremely difficult
because, in my heart of hearts, I knew college was a
mistake from the outset for me. I shared a room with an
extremely bubbly P.E. student called Joe. She constantly
ran everywhere, eating almost continually to keep up her
strength. One of her first comments to me was,
"Hey, you don't eat much do you? And you look a bit
thin. We'll have to do something about that."

In the next room lived Emma, a first year student. Emma
was a very pleasant girl and during the early days we
spent all of our spare time together, visiting different
parts of London. We were inseparable.

The first year of Sociology turned out to be a repeat of
my 'A' Level year, so I quickly changed courses to
Education. Emma was doing the same course, so it felt

safe having a friend alongside me. I liked the idea of perhaps becoming an infant school teacher, like my Mum, one day. I'd always enjoyed helping in the infants' school, teaching little children to read. During the first couple of weeks at college, I was very lonely and homesick and wanted to leave. It was only Emma who always convinced me to stay, saying if I left she would be totally lost herself. In those early weeks however I really missed my family and my old familiar surroundings. To beat the loneliness, I wrote dozens of letters to my parents and some old school friends. They all wrote back encouraging me.

There was one exception.

Why I wrote to my Grandmother I will never know.

Her letter back was poisonous.

"Dear Anna

The only good part about you going to college is that at least your parents have got you out of the way. They never wanted you in the first place. You're wasting your time at college. You'll never learn anything. You'll never succeed at anything. Fat, stupid children grow up to be fat, stupid students. Stop wasting your time and come home.

Gran."

Looking back now, I wonder why I never told anyone about this letter but as with all Gran's cruelty, her intimidation kept me quiet.

Instead of tearing it up, I read it repeatedly and for some masochistic reason I couldn't put it down.

For the first month, I decided not to go home for a weekend visit. I desperately wanted to become inaugurated into college life and make more friends. It was during the second week however that I phoned Dad at work, arranging to meet him for lunch.

Those two hours together were the happiest of my entire life. We ate in his local pub then walked round the Cut, an area of London with outdoor market stalls. My Father linked arms with me the whole time and I felt so safe. It was like I was meeting him for the first time and I loved him more than ever. It was very difficult when it was time for me to leave. I wanted to stay with Dad so much. I felt like a little girl again. As we parted that afternoon, he looked at me and said,
"Why do we put up with that woman?"
I cried as he walked away. Mum told me much later that he arrived home that night upset and continually talked about our lunch together.

A couple of weeks later I returned home for the weekend but with Gran about the house, Dad was back to his usual distant self. Despite detesting college I was truly relieved, early the following Monday morning to leave Gran behind and return to my lodgings.

Thanks to Emma, I somehow carried on with the course and although still unhappy, began to settle in. I soon realised Emma had many problems of her own. She was very plump and her Mum constantly told her to diet. I think, for Emma, my ability to refuse food was a major source of annoyance. Whereas she always ate too much, here I was, managing to refuse food with total ease.

I soon discovered she had the habit of buying food and secretly eating it in her room. Often I would enter to find a large selection of empty wrappers strewn across the floor. One night I couldn't sleep and seeing Emma's light on went in to find her sitting up in bed, surrounded by chocolate bars. With her mouth totally full, she couldn't speak. I left. Whenever we ate together, she first wolfed down her own meal then finished off anything left on my plate. On my birthday, my parents sent me a very expensive box of chocolates and, as usual, forever trying to please people, I gave them to Emma. Acting strangely, she opened them, ate one and then hysterically threw the rest of the box across the room, saying they were disgusting.

When we first met, Emma was always so kind but as time passed it seemed everything I did irritated her. Inevitably she spent a lot of time in her room sulking and our friendship seemed to cool. I felt very exposed one day, when she asked me if maybe I was anorexic. I dismissed the charge instantly and left the room with her shouting out after me,
"Well, are you anorexic? Are you?"

Emma was desperate to have a boyfriend and though there were so few boys at our college, she was always jealous when I got any attention.

As the weeks passed Emma grew more distant. She was no longer her usual chirpy self. Her comments concerning my weight and stature seemed to increase and instead of being jokey, they now were sharp and hurtful. The thinner I got, the more offensive and objectionable Emma became.

When we were out clothes shopping one day in Oxford Street, I was having trouble finding a pair of jeans to fit because I had now lost so much weight. I didn't even fit into the smallest size 8. I was upset and quite innocently asked Emma what I should do. Her response hit me where it hurt most. In the middle of the store, she started to shout,

"How should I know what you should do? I'm not the thin one. I'm fat and revolting, aren't I? Why are you always trying to make me feel so bad about my weight? You and your skinny, stick thin legs."

A tremendous feeling of guilt swept over me but before I could apologise, she'd stormed out of the shop and had vanished. I felt so alone and rejected once again. It took me a long time to compose myself before I wandered back to college alone.

That night in my room, for the first time ever, I cut my arms. They weren't deep cuts but I felt I deserved the pain because I'd upset Emma. I had discovered the best way to escape the mental anguish was by inflicting physical pain on myself. This mutilation, which I now call self-harming, was to continue for many years to come. To this day parts of my body still bear nothing but scars. As I cut myself, I heard the voice as clear as crystal, saying:

"Cut yourself! Cut yourself!"

The voice grew louder and louder sending me into an angry frenzy. Now hating myself so much, I must have cut myself at least thirty times. Eventually the red mist in my head cleared, the voice quietened and I stopped cutting myself.

Over the next few weeks, I did try to talk to Emma but she totally ignored me.

Throughout my college days, food remained a major issue for me. All my fellow students ate what seemed to me to be huge portions. I stuck rigidly to certain rules though, for example, I would never eat any potatoes or potato based products. Whereas the others piled their plates with boiled, fried or roast potatoes, I just had protein and vegetables.

The sad thing is, at this time I really felt very fat, not seeing the reality of exactly how much weight I'd already lost. I was now under 7 stones (98 lbs.). One day in the Social Biology class, we were all asked to feed in information about our weight and height into a computer for a project. It was now I was given factual computerised evidence of how emaciated I had become. Even I was shocked. The computer wouldn't accept my weight, it kept rejecting the figure I entered, stating repeatedly:
"Your weight is too low."
My individual experiment had to be abandoned but, what would have been disconcerting to other people, to me was so wonderful. I felt delighted, seeing my weight had fallen to an all time low. At that time everyone else in my class was always encouraging me to eat more but I was on a winning streak. I was losing weight and I didn't

want to stop. I always wanted to lose just one more pound.

Over the following weeks I became very depressed with my life at college and that Easter, when I went home for the holidays, I was at an all time low. Food totally preoccupied my thoughts now. I was given some Easter Eggs but I obviously couldn't eat any. Still, I gazed at them longingly. I could smell the rich chocolate through the wrappers and my empty stomach started to rumble again. During my stay at home, I had intended to start revising for the end of term exams but throughout the holidays was unable to concentrate. My body was starving and now I could think of nothing but food.

As the holiday's ended, I started to worry about the exams. I was also extremely apprehensive about meeting with Emma again. We hadn't spoken since that day in the shop in Oxford Street. She had avoided me constantly and would deliberately sit on the other side of the room during our lectures. When I returned to the flat after the break, I did go to her room but seeing me, she slammed the door, screaming,
"Go away, you skinny little bitch!"
That was the last time I ever saw Emma.

On the morning of the final exam, I felt extremely nervous knowing I hadn't revised properly. I sat down in the examination room thinking only of food and my weight. Since the test lasted three hours, we were all allowed to take food into the room with us. All the other students had bags overflowing with chocolate bars and sweets - in my bag was one small green apple. We settled at our desks as the exam papers were handed out. It was

12 o'clock and the exam began. My stomach started rumbling and I tensed my muscles trying to stop the noise, which sounded so loud in that silent room. Looking down at my bag, I instinctively reached for the apple. As I touched the smooth surface I realised what I was about to do and withdrew my hand as if I'd just touched something burning hot. What was I thinking? I couldn't eat anything! Where was my will power?

Turning over the first page of the test paper, I stared at the questions. I had to concentrate hard to stop them blurring before my eyes. I began writing down numbers, trying to calculate exactly how many calories I had eaten over the past week. No longer did I seem to have any control over my actions. The more figures I wrote on the page, the more panicky I felt inside, wanting the final total to be zero calories.

"Why do I ever have to eat anything?" I thought.

Glancing up at the clock, I saw twenty minutes had already passed and suddenly I was shocked back into the real world again. What was I doing? I was supposed to be answering the exam questions, not working out calories.

I was starving. My stomach being so empty, felt as though it was trying to eat itself, in fact it was. Once more I reached for the apple and this time placed it on my desk where I could see it. I wanted to eat that apple so much but I couldn't. The voice was shouting loud and clear in my head.

"Don't eat! Don't eat!"

I started to answer the questions on the exam paper again. Time was passing fast. It was now 2.00 p m. and I'd only just finished half the paper. My mind just wouldn't stay focused. Every now and then I realised, instead of writing an essay, I was still jotting down the calorific values of food. Another 50 minutes passed and the adjudicator announced there were only ten minutes to go. I had to pull myself together. I had to write, stay focused and forget about food for just this brief period of time.

After the exam I could hardly remember what I had written.

But I was proud. I knew I'd passed.

Not the exam, but the ultimate test.

I still hadn't eaten the apple! I proudly placed it back into my bag, along with my pens, feeling triumphant. I had endured excruciating hunger pains for three hours but came out victorious.

The voice congratulated me.

I was given my starvation diploma.

I was a success!

With the final exam finished, I went to my room to pack. I took everything I owned; something told me I would never return again. I left a note in the office for the Principal, saying I was finishing with college altogether.

On the train back to Southend I started to feel strange. By this time I hadn't eaten for over 30 hours and my head felt woozy. At Southend Station I was met on the platform by my parents, who were obviously shocked at my appearance. Once home however, nothing had changed. Mum just went to bed early and Dad soon joined her, leaving me alone with my Grandmother.

I knew Gran was about to start on me, and quickly went to bed, blocking the door with a chair.

Some weeks later I received my exam results. Nervously I slipped the letter into my pocket and walked down to Leigh Cliffs, certain I'd failed. Sitting on a bench, looking out to sea, I finally plucked up the courage and opened the envelope.

I couldn't believe my eyes. I had passed. But how?

I was amazed.

My lecturer had also written, pleading with me to reconsider my plans to leave.

I stared at the letter and then looked back out to sea. I just couldn't return to Whitelands and would get a job instead.

I tore the paper up, ending another chapter of my life.

Chapter 6

MY FIRST AND LAST JOB

At the age of nineteen, I started work as an office junior at Frankel Thurston and Co, a prominent local firm of solicitors. On my first morning in September I was ready hours in advance, feeling so nervous.

My first day at work seemed to be a bit of a blur. I met so many different people and was taught so many new skills. Initially I was a bit overwhelmed but it soon turned out that the job was pretty basic, not requiring a tremendous amount of intelligence. The work was mostly common sense and my colleagues were amazed at the speed at which I did everything. I enjoyed my job enormously and whenever I was set a task, I did it competently. Within days my responsibilities increased.

During the first few weeks I was very happy because the stress levels of this position were quite low. On my daily trips to Leigh Post Office it was like I was being let out of school again. The other secretaries usually asked me to pick up their sandwiches, which I was glad to do. When, at the end of the first month, I was handed a pay cheque, it felt as though I was being paid for enjoying myself.

Soon it became known I had secretarial skills and one day, when one of the secretaries was ill, Mr Frankel asked me to take some dictation. As he dictated the first letter I was shaking. I took down the shorthand, terrified I wouldn't be able to read back my outlines. Mr Frankel however was delighted with my work. The following Monday he called me into his office again. Only five weeks after being hired as an office junior he was now asking me if I would like to become a secretary. Deep down I would have been happier to stay as the office junior but I knew this was a good opportunity for promotion and I accepted.

In November Mr Frankel took on another legal executive, Tim Wilson. Tim had officially retired from a job in London at the age of 70 but a divorce very late in life left him with financial problems and he needed, once more, to earn a wage. During the first week his work was typed by the other executive's secretaries but it soon became obvious he really needed his own typist. Mr Frankel decided the best solution would be for me to start working as Tim's secretary in the mornings, and in the afternoons, carry on with my office junior duties. Rather foolishly, I agreed. In effect I was taking on two jobs. I was expected to do all Tim's typing and complete my junior tasks as well.

A new desk, chair and typewriter were bought for me and set up at the end of what was known as The Greenhouse. I was really quite proud and very excited at the prospect of having my own desk and typewriter. The company operated in a very old building and to make more space, they'd had a lean-to built onto the secretary's general office many years previously. It was made almost entirely of glass, hence the name Greenhouse. It wasn't the most comfortable of places to work because in the winter, it was freezing cold and in the summer, boiling hot. The glass extension was also pretty rickety, so during heavy storms it didn't feel terribly safe to be out there. In bad weather conditions Mr Frankel would stop me working, moving me to another position in the office. He treated me more like a daughter, always asking if everything was all right.

I don't know if it was just the increased work pressure but after a few months of feeling better, my anorexic behaviour began all over again. The anorexic voice in my head treated me like a slave, demanding each day I drove myself harder and ate less.

"You're not losing weight fast enough. I am making five new rules for you. I am going to tell you what you have to do:-

1. *Do your work perfectly with no mistakes.*
2. *Never eat a biscuit.*
3. *Cut your calories down by 100 to 800 calories a day.*
4. *Do one extra hours exercise a day.*
5. *Only drink water during the day and nothing else."*

I'd never had any specific legal training. Typing a will or contract isn't easy as it has to be perfect, there can be no margin of error. I worked flat out every morning to complete Tim's work. Then in the afternoon I swapped hats, leaving behind the complex mental work to run around completing the much more physically demanding junior work. All the other secretaries saved their photocopying and other boring tasks for me to do in the afternoons, making everything that much harder. Fitting two full-time jobs into one day proved hard; soon the pressure began to affect me. Instead of admitting this to Mr Frankel, which I could have so easily done when he asked how I was managing, I just said everything was fine.

This passive behaviour was because I had always wanted to be liked by other people. I had been indoctrinated by my Grandmother, from an early age, to regard myself as a piece of rubbish. When anybody praised me, in any way, I just couldn't understand it. One day, an electrician came to the office to repair a light. Clare, Mr Frankel's secretary, introduced us.

"This is Anna", she said. "She'll show you the problem."

I was amazed by the reaction I received. The electrician smiled and said,

"Wow, you're Anna. You're so gorgeous I'd do anything for you."

I was very embarrassed by his comment and as soon as I had shown him the broken light, scurried away. Desperate for love and attention, I hugged his words to my heart for days. This man actually thought that I was attractive. I still couldn't believe what I had heard. Gran had always convinced me from a very young age that I was an ugly person.

By Christmas of that year, I was mentally and physically drained. I was going to apply for leave over the Christmas period but was told by one of the secretaries this would be impossible because of the volume of work the firm had outstanding. I desperately needed a break and, as it was traditional in my family for everyone to be home for the two Christmas weeks, my Mother suggested I tell a white lie. Why not say we were going away for Christmas and that the holiday had been booked long before I started work? I felt extremely uncomfortable about lying but knew if I didn't get some rest, I was going to collapse anyway. I explained the situation to Mr Frankel who was very understanding, which made me feel even worse about making up the story. Southend is a small town and now I was very unsure about whether I'd be able to go out anywhere during my Christmas holiday. What if I bumped into a member of the staff?

But even before my holiday, there was another major hurdle to overcome. The firm's Christmas Lunch.

As part of his Christmas bonus every year, Mr Frankel paid for a three-course meal at a very expensive local restaurant. Just the idea of this scared me stiff. How would I manage to eat a reasonable amount of food? Would everyone comment about how little I was eating? I didn't drink. I just never liked the taste of alcohol. Socialising with the partners would be unbearable because I only ever spoke to Mr Frankel, or the other solicitors, on a professional level. What would they want to talk about? Would I appear stupid? Then there was the big question of what to wear.

Mr Frankel gave everyone a day off in December to allow them to do their Christmas shopping. I spent my day with Mum going into every shop in Basildon, looking for a dress suitable to wear to the dreaded lunch. Eventually I found one I thought was acceptable. On the day though I felt terribly self-conscious in that ridiculous white dress.

My mother always dealt with stress by taking another tranquilliser and it was that day Mum decided I should do the same. It wasn't necessary for me to contact Dr Chambers for a prescription though because with strict instructions not to mention it to Dad, Mum became the doctor and dispensed me the pills from her own stock. Over the following months, every time I looked depressed, Mum insisted I took another tranquilliser. I didn't like the effect and pretended to be taking the pills when in fact, I was hiding them. It even reached the stage where I would act as though I was tranquillised and sedated in front of Mum just to please her.

The lunch turned out to be a nightmare. We left the office at 1.00 pm and all piled into various cars. By this time I was feeling spaced out on Mum's tranquillisers and my whole body was shaking. Food terrified me. How on earth was I going to eat a whole meal? When we walked into the restaurant, Mr Frankel was already there to greet us. He asked me what I wanted to drink. Even though I never touched alcohol I found it impossible, as usual, to say no. I heard Clare ordering a sweet sherry and said I would have one too. When I took a tiny sip of this strange deep red liquid the taste shocked me. It tasted horrible.

After about twenty minutes we were told our table was ready and staying close to Clare, I walked across the room. Slipping into a seat right at the end of a table I cunningly, switched my full sherry glass with Clare's almost empty one. I sighed in relief seeing Mr Frankel and Tim were right at the other end of the table.
"Thank goodness I won't have to talk with them", I thought to myself.
Then the menus were handed out. I stared at mine in horror. My hands started to shake and the menu slipped out of my grasp and crashed onto the table, knocking several glasses over. I was so embarrassed!

The food arrived - mountains of turkey, roast potatoes, Yorkshire pudding, Brussel sprouts, carrots, peas, it never ended. The sight of so much food sent me into a panic. It seemed all those enormous silver dishes were floating towards me. Excusing myself I ran to the ladies toilet weeping. I must have stayed there for ages because eventually Clare came looking for me. She escorted me back to the table, where under strict instructions from the voice, I announced I'd been sick and couldn't eat a thing.

Suddenly I felt so wonderful, so proud.

I'd done it! I'd done it!

Christmas lunch! With all my fellow workers and yes, I had come through on zero calories!

My white dress seemed quite pretty now.

"Wow, if I could do that, I could do anything", I thought as Mr Frankel wished us all a Happy Christmas.
I left the restaurant and walked home on a high.

Zero calories for Christmas lunch.

"How many people can achieve that?" I said to myself.

I didn't have a very good Christmas, though. Did I ever? Every year since I was a small child, I'd been ill during Christmas. My parents had, in the past, believed it to be the result of too much excitement. But as always the real reason was my Grandmother.

We always went round to my Grandmother's on Christmas Day and as I grew older I became more averse to these visits. Each year my body told itself to be ill, then I wouldn't have to go to Gran's. I was quite genuinely ill. Over the years I had bronchitis or flu's with high temperatures, anything that would force me to stay home in bed. Every Christmas my parents were mystified when, once again, I wasn't well.

As usual, during the Christmas period of 1987, I spent most of the holiday in bed. This year I had fresh worries about returning to work in January. The only good news was it had been a good Christmas calorie wise. Following the firm's Christmas lunch I had managed to eat practically nothing all over Christmas.

Early in January I returned to work with all its problems. Superficially Tim, my boss, appeared to be a very sweet man, always chatting and joking with the other staff. However, alone with me he behaved differently. Tim knew this was my first job but instead of making any allowances, he came down on me heavily every time I made a mistake. He would stand at the entrance to The Greenhouse shouting,
"How do you spell the word 'litigation'?"
Instead of just pointing out a spelling mistake to me, Tim took delight in his public ridicule. Once again I felt a complete failure. I couldn't even spell simple words correctly any more. My insecurity made me forget my 39 perfectly typed letters, and I focused solely on the one mistake.

Another pattern began to develop. Tim started to call me into his office for shorthand dictation, where previously he had used a tape recorder. I soon realised Tim only called me in when I was wearing a short skirt. Since we were only allowed to wear skirts to work I had bought about an equal number of long and short ones. Soon it became apparent Tim didn't call me into his room when I was wearing a long skirt. I felt dirty and sitting there with my legs tightly crossed I still felt him looking up my skirt. I hated being alone with Tim, feeling physically sick whenever he put his arm around my shoulder. At first I tried to convince myself Tim was only trying to be friendly - but who was I trying to fool? Tim humiliated me at every opportunity. He was just a dirty old man. As usual, I thought I deserved this man's abuse and didn't have the self-respect to tell anyone what was happening.

As the months passed, I became severely depressed.

My weight had plummeted and my clothes were now beginning to hang on me.

Anorexia was my safe escape in times of trouble.

I tried for a while to take a packed lunch down to Leigh Cliffs but the anorexic voice soon told me to throw it away.

"Throw that food in the sea. It will make you fat", the voice screamed above the ocean breeze.

I threw the food into the waves and watched it sink. For the rest of the time, in the lunch hours I used to wander aimlessly around Leigh, staring through shop windows at fashionable clothes, dreaming of being thin enough to fit into those tiny garments. The irony being, if I had actually tried on any of these 'tiny' clothes they would have swamped me, for now my weight had dropped to well below seven stones (98 lbs.).

I saw couples walking hand in hand and felt so lonely and sad as I watched them smile, giggle and reach out for each other. My Grandmother had always told me I would never have a boyfriend. Even though I was desperate to feel the warmth and security of a loving relationship, I hated my body and knew that any relationship would eventually become physical. As much as I wanted the comfort and reassurance of a man's touch, I couldn't allow anyone to find out just how fat I actually was under my clothes.

It was around this time, I discovered the perfect way for me to have a relationship without physical contact. The answer was easy. Do it all by post. This way the boy would never actually see me and discover how fat and ugly I really was under my clothes.

It was through a pen club I met Pete and we began writing to each other.

Pete, a Graphics Designer for the Navy, lived in Portsmouth. From his photo I could see he was handsome, with short dark wavy hair. He owned his own house and car. He soon started to ask if he could drive down to visit me but this worried me a lot and I didn't know what to do. I liked him very much but I was scared of him at the same time. After writing to each other for several months, he sent me my first ever Valentine's card but I just couldn't let him visit. I knew he would probably want a physical relationship. At 21 I hadn't even kissed a boy yet, let alone had sex. I just couldn't take my clothes off in front of another person. Deeply ashamed of my body, I was too afraid to let it go further and wrote to him insisting he stopped writing. He did write a few more letters but as I never replied, he took the hint and stopped.

I didn't consciously decide to stop eating again. This time it all happened slowly and gradually without me actually realising. I found work a scary and nerve-wracking place and I was forever waiting for a new attack from Tim. I began to feel physically sick as I entered the office and this feeling lasted all day. Afraid I would throw up at work, I virtually stopped eating during office hours. My lunch was now one packet of low calorie crisps. I avoided the other secretaries, particularly during the breaks because they would have Kit-Kats with their coffee and biscuits throughout the morning from a tin they kept under the post desk.

My health was bad by now, very bad. I felt extremely low and drained of all energy. Though I suspected I was suffering from Anorexia nervosa, I constantly asked myself what this disease was all about. Desperate for more information, on my way home one evening, I stopped at a bookshop, searching for a book on eating disorders. Sadly I was unable to find anything. While I was in the shop, an assistant approached me asking if I wanted any help but I left the shop in a panic. What was I going to do? Ask for a book on anorexia?

A day or so later, I found a medical book on anorexia advertised in a catalogue from a Book Club. That same night I stayed up long after my parents had gone to bed, writing the letter ordering the book, insisting it was sent to me in a plain envelope. Two weeks later a small parcel arrived. I took it straight to my room. The more I read the more dumbfounded I became. The book was all about me. I was grossly underweight. I was cold all the time and had very bad circulation so my fingers were blue. I had soft downy hair all over my body. Every word described me exactly. I had all of the symptoms that were listed - there really was no doubting the facts.

I started to sweat. What if my parents discovered the book and put two and two together? They would force me to eat. Quickly I destroyed the book.

My life was becoming more frightening by the day. Each time I saw Mum and Dad watching the news I panicked. Sometimes there were reports about eating disorders. I was so very afraid that these programmes would trigger a realisation in my parents about the nature of their daughter's problems. I now did anything to keep anorexia from their minds. If there was something about this topic on television, I would deliberately spill something to divert their attention. I began checking all magazines and papers coming into the house for anorexia articles, destroying them before anyone had a chance to read them.

Clare was one of the girls from work that I got quite close to. She was about my age, tall and thin and had brown hair. She often saw me walking to the office. She always stopped to give me a lift. I felt terrible every time this happened, as though I was cheating on my slimming. Walking those four miles each day was a task the voice ordered me to complete. It was an incredible struggle but I wouldn't give up.

The anorexic voice told me to change my route so there would be no opportunity for Clare to see me.

"Walk that way and she won't spot you", the voice commanded.

Every time Clare spotted me and I accepted a lift, the voice made me pay a forfeit.

"You took a lift. Now pay the price and eat one less potato tonight."

I obeyed the voice, cutting down further on my daily intake. If I was having two small potatoes with my dinner, I would make sure that evening I had only one.

There is a major difficulty that comes when an anorexic cuts out any item of food. Having been removed, it then becomes impossible to return this food to your daily diet. Once I had reduced the potatoes from two to one, it was irreversible. From that day onwards, I only ever had one potato with my evening meal. It wasn't long before I was eating very little indeed.

It was around this time that the voice really started to take over. As a torture, it drew me repeatedly back to look in bakeries and grocery shop windows.

"Lovely cakes but you don't deserve any", the voice would whisper.

The only way I was eating now was through my eyes. An anorexic is always hungry. It's like a life long punishment. You want to eat all the time but won't allow yourself. I stood for ages outside cake shops, mentally devouring the rows of delicious looking pastries so tantalisingly displayed.

Two days before Christmas, I collapsed. This time my body had decided it'd really had enough. I went down with a bad bout of flu. I was grateful at first, as it allowed me to miss that year's firm's Christmas Lunch. After a week, there was no improvement and I realised something else was amiss. The New Year was nearly upon us and I had to return to work. Now I was very thin, pale and tired. The facade I'd somehow kept up for so many years was finally slipping.

Early in January, although sick, I stubbornly returned to work and battled on through that first week. Tim had masses of work for me but I just struggled through. By the Friday it was very obvious to everyone I couldn't cope. I now looked as pale as a ghost and my eyes, huge and deep-set, had black shadows beneath them. Mr Frankel came to my desk at the end of the day, telling me how concerned he felt. I didn't look strong enough to stand up, let alone work full-time at such a very demanding job. He had a very generous proposal for me.
"Anna, you've worked very well here and we value you as an employee but you don't look at all well. You really do look weak and under the weather", he said. "How would you like to work mornings only for a while? Then you could go home at one o'clock, rest for a while and re-charge your batteries for the next day."

I was very weak now and, relieved, agreed to only work half a day. I really hadn't enough strength to walk four miles each day, as well as type complicated leases. Having the afternoons off didn't really help because by eating less and less, I wasn't regaining any strength whatsoever.

I was now seeing my G.P. regularly on a fortnightly basis. By this time, he had become extremely concerned over my health and now concentrated solely on my weight.
"You are far too thin", he kept saying.

It was obvious to everyone that though I was only working mornings, my health wasn't improving in any way. My doctor was becoming very concerned about the continued weight loss and made an appointment for me at Southend General Hospital.

A few days later, I visited the chief psychiatrist, Dr Lintell.

I didn't want them to, but Mum and Dad came with me.

Dr Lintell was quite an elderly lady, around 70 years old. Initially she talked mostly to my parents but I was forced to answer a few questions briefly when they were directed at me.

"How much did I weigh?"
"I'm not exactly sure."

"Was I having periods?"
"No."

"What did I eat during the day?"

"Lots and lots."

"How much exercise did I do?"
"None at all."

At first the questions were answered by me but gradually, as the interview progressed, I gave way entirely to the anorexic voice who lied as it dealt with all the answers. After a while I couldn't hear the questions any more and it felt like I'd left the room. Everybody was talking and the noise got louder and louder, until suddenly there was total silence for a few moments.

Dr Lintell then turned to me and said:

"Anna, you have Anorexia nervosa."

Her words made me feel as though I had a one way ticket and couldn't stop the train.

My parents, who probably knew all along, were now shocked to hear a doctor confirm that their daughter officially had Anorexia nervosa.

Mum and Dad stepped in at this point and made the decision for me. I wasn't strong enough to return to work.

I was stunned. I wanted to go back to work and act as though nothing had happened but was somewhat relieved when Dad phoned Mr Frankel. He was very understanding and said I should not worry - he would keep my job open for me for as long as it took for me to recover.

A few days later, I went alone to the office to collect my things. I felt very emotional seeing the desk and typewriter that had been bought especially for me. On the desk was a huge furry teddy bear and an enormous card. The entire office had signed it with loving messages. Emptying my desk, in the bottom drawer, I found a weight readout card from the local pharmacy. It read "Your weight is 7 stones 10 pounds (108 lbs.)" and was dated six months previously.

"Oh God", I thought, feeling huge. "I must be so much heavier now. Why, oh why couldn't I have kept to that weight? Why did I allow myself to get fat again?"

The other secretaries were all calling to say goodbye but I felt so fat and, not wanting them to see me, rushed out of my office. By the front door Tim grabbed me, pressing himself up against me. Somehow breaking free, I found myself in the street. All this man ever was, was a male version of my Grandmother.

Clutching the teddy bear, I raced quickly round the corner to the local pharmacy to weigh myself. I ran into the pharmacy and practically leapt onto the scales.

The five-second pause on the weighing machine seemed to last forever, then out came the printed ticket with my weight.

It read "7 stones 11 pounds (109 lbs.)" I was horrified. I was putting on weight.

Sitting the teddy bear on the floor, I put in another coin, looking again at the first ticket.

Suddenly I was overcome with joy. I had read the first ticket incorrectly. It really said, "6 stones 11 pounds (91 lbs.)" I weighed nearly a stone less.

Seconds later the other ticket came out reading the same. I cuddled the teddy bear tightly.
"If only I could be like you", I thought, "and weigh nothing."

I felt amazing as I slowly walked home, as though I was walking on air. Immediately I started planning.

If I could lose 13 lbs. in six months, then I could lose more weight. I had to diet even more strictly. I'd start tonight.

HIDING MYSELF UNDER BAGGY
CLOTHES

Chapter 7

OFFICIALLY DIAGNOSED ANOREXIC

I woke at 6.00 am Monday morning, with the alarm ringing, and got out of bed. Only after a few minutes did I suddenly realise there was no more work to go to.

Nothing to get dressed for. Nothing to be on time for. Nothing to worry about. Nothing to succeed at.

Nothing.

People would no longer say, "You look thin."

People would no longer say, "You look ill."

People would no longer say, "You've lost weight."

Now the world knew I had Anorexia nervosa.

My official label of Anorexia nervosa was my final cry for help. There was a sense of relief but also a sense of guilt.

This guilt was reinforced on Thursday during my first appointment with the psychiatrist Dr Lintell.

Without my knowledge, the previous day, my Mother had seen Doctor Lintell as a private patient. In many ways, my Mother was always just as ill as me. After all, my Grandmother was her Mother and she has abused her daughter, my Mother, as a child. Exactly what my Mother actually told the Doctor I will never know but what followed was beyond belief.

Doctor Lintell sat me down very officially and, like a strict headmistress, informed me it was my Anorexia nervosa that had caused Mum's illness. That doctor laid into me unmercifully, saying I should pull myself together. Just go home and eat, then everybody would get better.

"Do you want to make your Mother ill?" she asked.

My Mother's addiction to tranquillisers started when I was six years old and couldn't be my fault. Was what happened to me between the ages of six and thirteen influenced by my parents? Shouldn't they now accept some responsibility? Why was my Mother now pointing the finger at me?

It was at the end of my first official week at home as a diagnosed anorexic, when a new family illness occurred. This time it wasn't mine. Halfway through the day, Mum came into the lounge, saying she didn't feel well. Lying on the couch next to me, she began acting very strangely, complaining of how terribly cold she felt inside. Absolutely terrified, she asked me to ring the doctor and get him round quickly. I phoned the doctor, then called Dad, who said he would come home immediately. Back in the lounge, I found Mum was now lying on the floor, staring into space. I desperately tried to talk with her but she wouldn't respond to anything I said and by now, I was extremely scared.

Here I was, classified as an official anorexic, now being employed as head nurse to my Mum, who I later found out was actually suffering from the withdrawal symptoms of tranquillisers. My Mother had been addicted to tranquillisers, in heavy doses, for seventeen years. Recently she'd seen a programme on TV about the side effects and dangers of long term use. The report frightened her and panicking, without telling anyone, she'd stopped a life long pill taking habit overnight. She was now experiencing cold turkey, in at the deep end.

When Dad came home, the doctor still wasn't there so together, we helped Mum upstairs to bed. Eventually, an hour later, the doctor arrived.

Dr Chambers had now retired and Dr Lee was our new family GP. He was a short Asian man, far stricter than Dr Chambers when it came to prescribing tranquillisers. The new doctor refused to prescribe Mum any of the usual tranquillisers, putting her instead on a very mild medication. For over ten minutes, my Mother pleaded for the old tranquillisers but there was no compromising. The doctor bluntly refused to be coerced.

Mum started taking the new medication but it didn't help her condition at all. She remained terrified, staying upstairs in bed for days just rocking back and forth, staring into space.

With Mum ill and me just diagnosed with anorexia, Dad now decided to have time off work and take charge of things.

Dad didn't really have any idea about the quantity of food I should have been eating. He was starting totally from scratch, not having cooked before.

It was pointless asking me, an anorexic, what I should eat. I would have just lied so I could eat as little as possible. My Father decided a reasonable breakfast for me, each day, was two Weetabix with milk. This was certainly not an excessive or unreasonable amount for an adult person but just the thought of it filled me with fear. Every morning when I awoke, it was the first thing in my head. I would look into the bowl in sheer panic. Had Dad put more milk in the dish than yesterday? Was there more sugar on top? As he handed me the breakfast each morning, I always started to shake and couldn't stop crying, desperately trying to eat the cereal.

It seemed to me that I'd only just managed to deal with breakfast when lunch was upon us. Dad's meals were quite simple really, consisting of boiled eggs with soldiers, fish and chips from the local shop or just about anything with instant mashed potatoes. However, considering he had Mum to look after as well upstairs in bed, my Father really did a brilliant job.

As each meal time approached, my anxiety levels grew until, within a short time, I reached a state of near hysteria every time I sat down to eat.

Eating anything now had become a major event. My way of behaving around food had changed dramatically and the plate of food had to look a certain way before I was able to start. I needed to see blank spaces between the food and it had to be only one layer thick. I only ate tiny pieces of food at a time and became an expert at judging portion sizes. I would know for certain if there was one pea extra on my plate.

As the fears raged away inside me, the number of foods I considered 'safe' continued to decrease until my diet was restricted to very few foods. To me, 'safe' foods were those containing the fewest calories.

I was now totally obsessed with being thin, and daily my mind became more like a calculator, working out the number of calories in every bite I took. I added up my score, even if I only ate a slice of melon. I was terrified that I would exceed 600 calories. Like a college professor, I studied calorie books day and night. I became a walking food encyclopaedia. If you told me a weight and named a food, within seconds I could tell you the exact calorie count.

We had reached the last few days before Christmas and the situation at home was getting worse. Mum was still acting strangely all the time and my Grandmother was constantly at our house. This all left me in a hopeless state of depression. With my insides aching, I started experiencing serious thoughts of suicide. I'd had enough. I really wanted to die.

My bizarre ambition was to be dead before I was forced to eat Christmas lunch. Killing myself became very real. I planned to buy a Stanley knife and cut my wrists while I was in a hot bath. The idea of cutting myself didn't scare me so much. Dying began to really look all quite simple to me.

The next morning my Mother was going shopping with
Gran and as soon as they'd gone, I sneaked out to the
local DIY shop and bought my death knife. Back at
home, I felt amazingly relaxed as I ran the hot bath.
Locking the door, I climbed into the bath, saying a prayer
whilst looking for my major vein. Killing yourself is a
hard job and, very frightened, I began to tremble. Finally
I cut myself, and although I missed the main vein, the cut
was quite deep and blood began to pour from my wrist.
As the bath water changed to red, I began crying
hysterically. Thinking I was about to die, I panicked and
jumped out the bath. I ran into my bedroom and
bandaged my wrist tightly to stop the bleeding. An hour
or so later, I calmed down and got off the bed.

Luckily Mum and Gran were still out, giving me time to
clean the bath, hiding all the evidence. They, like the rest
of the world, were oblivious to my torment on that lonely
morning.

Christmas arrived but we hardly celebrated it. Everyone
was so down and sad. Mum's condition worsened once
more and now she wouldn't leave the house, even to visit
our closest relatives. At this stage Dad wasn't coping too
well either and he always panicked when Mum was ill.
His natural reaction to any difficult situation was always
to go to sleep. It is as if my Father's body just shuts down
and says "Look I really can't manage. I've had enough.
I'm going to escape and go to sleep." Every year we had a
real Christmas tree in the lounge that Dad took
tremendous trouble to decorate. That year, Dad had
bought an extra big tree in the hope that a festive
atmosphere might help with the family mood.

Ironically, it seemed even the Christmas tree couldn't cope. On Christmas Day afternoon, half way through the Queen's speech the tree slowly fell sideways to the floor. It was as if everything and everyone was giving up. As I listened to Queen Elizabeth on the television saying, "As we reflect back on the year..." I looked over to see Dad, asleep on the couch. Mum was upstairs, dead to the world. Mark was in his bedroom, counting his fish. Suddenly there was a banging on the front door. Someone had put the safety catch on and my Grandmother couldn't get in. As ill as I was, I smiled to see Dad sleep through it all.

"Let me in, let me in!" my Grandmother screamed from the street.

"The only way you'll get in is if you come down the chimney", I thought to myself.

Christmas passed and six days later, as New Year came, everybody was roughly in the same position. Early in January, Mum was back on her miracle pills. She had somehow persuaded Dr Lintell to give her a private prescription for Librium. One hour after taking her first few tablets, Mum was back to health, in her familiar tranquillised state. Those 'Mother's Little Helpers' really brought our family once more together and with Mum on her feet again, Dad was very relieved. His wife was back in charge, freeing him once more to return to work.

Having finally cured one patient in our house, Dr Lintell could concentrate on the other patient, who was getting thinner by the day. A few days later, Dr Lintell wrote, saying a new psychiatric nurse, Jill, was to take charge of my case.

Chapter 8

PSYCHIATRIC TREATMENT AT HOME

I was very apprehensive meeting Jill, the new psychiatric nurse. I had imagined some strict old Victorian nurse, an extension of Gran. However, she was actually quite young and plump with short dark hair.

On the first of our weekly sessions, Jill explained what her role was to be. Her job was to establish if a psychological reason was at the root of all my troubles.
"Here we go", I thought. "I must avoid questions about my childhood at all costs."
Even at the age of twenty-one, I was still so afraid of reprisals from Gran.

During my initial counselling session with Jill, I didn't have to worry though because Mum joined us. My Mother took up practically the entire first hour, explaining in great detail the terrifying ordeal she herself had just experienced - her six weeks of tranquilliser withdrawal.

Jill became exasperated and eventually, just before the session finished, managed to shut Mum up. It was only for the last three or four minutes that we actually talked about me.

The visits continued, and for the first month, Jill concentrated on my background. Mum, who was always present at our sessions, answered most of the questions, giving her expert version of my life. My Mother went on and on to Jill about how tired I was, and this and other comments about my physical being, confused Jill. My Mother's interpretation probably misled Jill into thinking, as she soon did, that I was suffering from a physical illness rather than anorexia. Jill's questions concentrated on the amount of energy I had and how much exercise I was doing. She was more concerned with my energy level and how my muscles reacted to various exercises than anything to do with my eating habits.

Dr Lintell had categorically diagnosed me as anorexic. In her mind there was no doubt, but Jill had very different ideas. It wasn't very long before Jill totally disagreed with Dr Lintell's diagnosis altogether.

She believed I suffered from muscle weakness, chronic fatigue and loss of appetite, caused by a physical illness, which could be cured by rest. She was convinced I had chronic fatigue syndrome, otherwise known as M.E., not Anorexia nervosa.

Jill, adamant her M.E. diagnosis was correct, didn't believe Dr Lintell had spent anywhere near enough time with me, prior to making a diagnosis of anorexia. Jill agreed that anorexia and M.E. had similar symptoms - M.E. caused loss of appetite, tiredness and muscle pains but Jill could not see any evidence whatsoever of anorexia in my behaviour. Jill didn't know however about the laxatives that I was secretly taking.

As my diet diminished, like all anorexics, I became constipated and began to seriously abuse laxatives. At first, I only needed a couple of tablets a week but as the illness progressed, this escalated to seventeen at a time. The stomach pains were unbearable and I spent hours and hours emptying my body of everything I'd eaten. Whereas normal people would go to the toilet once a day, I would totally clear my system up to ten times each day.

Jill also did not think I was trying to avoid eating at all costs. Yes, she agreed, I was thin but Jill said this was because the M.E. made me feel sick and it was this M.E. that made me limit my diet.

With hindsight, I understand how easy it was for Jill to be misled. In front of my Mother, I was unable to talk in any way about my anorexic feelings. I found it totally impossible to express how terrified I was of eating.

It was impossible to talk freely about the abuse from my Grandmother or explain the reality of my food problem. With Mum always present, what chance did Jill ever have to get anywhere near the truth?

M.E. for me however was wonderful. Being able to say it was a physical illness meant it wasn't my fault any more. I had a physical illness, which I couldn't help. Nobody could be angry with me for being unlucky enough to become physically ill. M.E. made me feel less of a nuisance and was the perfect escape from the shame of my anorexia. It was a wonderful excuse because with M.E., everybody would now feel sorry for me. I was living a lie but under the cover of that lie, I could respectably stop eating.

Jill put forward her M.E. theory to Dr Lintell. The doctor was clearly uninterested in Jill's opinion. She said I was suffering with anorexia and this was the only illness Jill should treat me for. The doctor's short and sharp response annoyed Jill. Infuriated, she now wrote to Dr Lintell a second time, demanding a meeting between herself, Dr Lintell and Dr Lee.

The proposed meeting was like my own private showdown of medical opinions at the OK Corral.

Jill, Dr Lee and Mum, of course, attended the meeting. Dr Lintell herself was noticeably absent. She pulled out at the last minute, claiming she had another appointment. Jill was furious. She'd already convinced Dr Lee I had M.E. and with his backing, she wanted to show Dr Lintell her error in diagnosing me anorexic.

I have to take responsibility for not telling the truth and although at the time, I was very relieved to be diagnosed as having M.E., I now deeply regret it. Jill's misdiagnosis set back my recovery by years. The recovery rate for anorexics is very closely linked to the length of time before the illness is actually treated. If caught early, sufferers of eating disorders have a significantly higher recovery rate.

I now realise if Jill had followed Dr Lintell's original diagnosis and treated me for anorexia at the age of 21, this may have saved me many years of torment, preventing many of the complications only recently arising. Today I frequently have bouts of chronic anaemia. My blood count falls too low, often requiring urgent treatment. Without this treatment I could fall into a coma. My bone density is also greatly reduced down to only 70% in some parts of my body, which could easily lead to osteoporosis (brittle bone disease) as I grow older.

For the next six months Jill treated me for M.E., encouraging me to participate in gentle exercise, fully accepting that my continued weight loss was part and parcel of that illness. Exactly when Jill changed her mind and accepted the possibility of anorexia I don't know but as I got thinner and thinner, she began to have grave doubts about her own original M.E. diagnosis. Regardless of her new diet plan, I still was not putting on any weight at all and Jill became very worried. Up until then Dr Lee had weighed me once a month but now I'd reached a weight level where I was at risk of having a heart attack.

Six months passed and I was getting no better. Jill became increasingly concerned. Ultimately I was Jill's responsibility and it was now that she decided to monitor the whole situation more closely. In future she would weigh me herself, twice a week on Mondays and Fridays.

Jill had by now realised I wore different clothes every time I saw Dr Lee and was suspicious this affected my weight. Was I cheating in other ways? Did I carry weights in my pockets? The only way she'd ever find out was by weighing me herself.

It was after the first of Jill's weighing sessions that my parents decided they had to now become directly involved. Mum and Dad were not at all happy with Jill weighing me in private and keeping the confidential results to herself. My parents, feeling left out of the action, decided they would weigh me independently themselves once a week on a Sunday.

Now with me cheating by constantly wearing extra clothes, my weight was rising with Dr Lee, falling with Jill and fluctuating considerably with Mum and Dad.

The new weighing sessions with Mum and Dad were the worst and each Sunday morning I was terrified of even going downstairs. My parents, of course, were pleased if I'd put on weight but if I lost weight they always became very angry. Following a Sunday morning weight decrease, whole days would pass when they barely spoke to me. It was often Tuesday or Wednesday the following week before they would even acknowledge me again.

In actual fact, my true weight varied only marginally between March and November of 1990, though the trend was usually downwards. My weight was now only 6¼ stones (87 lbs.). If an anorexic can keep her weight below 7 stones (98 lbs.) she feels safe. An anorexic can, in her own eyes, never be thin enough. Her view of herself is permanently distorted. When she looks into a mirror all she sees is a fat body and even when I was 6¼ stones (87 lbs.), I still thought that I should be thinner.

Around December, as my weight had fallen again, Dr Lee began to issue me with more ultimatums. If my weight didn't increase, he would insist I was to be hospitalised immediately.

The situation was deteriorating. Dr Lee spoke with my parents, agreeing as a last resort that Mum and Dad totally oversaw everything I ate.

My parents were now officially in charge. Each meal time became a battle of wits, as I started to learn new and deceitful ways of managing not to eat.

I realised when I was eating with my parents that they were concentrating on their meals, looking at their own food. We also always ate in the lounge whilst watching the television so when they were paying the least attention to me, I'd discreetly slip food into a handkerchief, later disposing of it down the toilet.

Very soon I became an expert at hiding food right under my parent's noses. I started wearing long sleeved jumpers allowing me, like a conjurer hiding his rabbit, to slip hankies filled with food up my sleeves. I always felt betrayed at dinner time because, having agreed the amount of food on my plate with my Mother, she always added extra, causing me additional terror and making it even harder for me to eat.

All this left me living constantly on the edge, always afraid each time I slipped food into my hanky, I'd been seen. It was ongoing pressure because even after I'd managed to hide the food, there was still a chance I'd be discovered before I had an opportunity to dispose of it.

This pattern continued for some time, until one day in September, Dad caught me red-handed, throwing away food. My ultimate nightmare had come true. I had been found out.

What next? A locked hospital?

It was all out in the open. I'd been caught and unable to look my parents in the eyes, I cried for the whole afternoon while they comforted me. Mum and Dad assured me that everything would be alright. Now my problems were out in the open, all I had to do was promise to stop hiding food and eat the meals they set out each day.

"Just eat the food we give you and it'll all be okay", Dad assured me.

What they didn't realise was, by this time, it wasn't me who decided what to eat.

It wasn't me that counted the calories.

It wasn't me that had to be thin.

It was the voice, and the voice wouldn't agree to my Father's request.

"Anna, go along with him. Let him believe you'll eat. Don't worry we'll find ways of cheating. I won't let you get fat."

Life is strange but at this, my lowest ebb, something quite dramatic happened in our quiet suburban household.

For as long as I could remember, we had a ritual each and every Sunday.

My Grandmother came round for Sunday tea.

It was always the same and it never varied. On the dot of 6.00 pm, we all sat down, round the same table, in the same corner, of the same room. The TV was always on with the same programme, Songs of Praise. We each sat on the same chairs, used the same china and in the middle of the table, stood the same cake dish with that week's new cake. Every week, as I stared at the cake, it turned into Gran's face, screaming.

"Eat me! Eat me!"

As I grew older, the voice in my head started shouting back.

"No cake! No cake!"

Why this week was different I'll never know. After all there had been over 1000 other Sunday teas but the next ten minutes changed all our lives quite dramatically.

My Grandmother always sat next to me, whispering her latest torment but that week I just couldn't hear her. I could see her lips moving but couldn't hear a single word. Getting no response, she began tapping me on the knee. Uncharacteristically, I went berserk and crying, ran out the room. I hid in my bedroom but Gran came up after me and held me down on the bed, shouting:
"You're fat! You're fat!"

Dad came to my bedroom and ordered my Grandmother out the room, telling her to leave. I stayed in my room but could hear everything being said.

There was an almighty bang as the door slammed. Gran had gone.

"Well?" Dad said to Mum.

"Well?" Mum replied.

"Well, I'll tell you what", Dad said. "We are moving, and moving as far away from that woman as we possibly can."

There was silence. I couldn't believe what I was hearing and waited for it all to start again, but not another word.

Just silence.

The following Sunday we all sat down. The TV was on, with Songs of Praise in the background. Five chairs - for me, my brother Mark, Mum and Dad and an empty chair.

The clock struck 6.00 pm and we all began our tea.

There was no Gran.

Just a cake that didn't talk.

Chapter 9

ESCAPING TO CORNWALL

Dad had the option of early retirement and, on the last day of June 1990, after working at Scotland Yard for over 30 years, he left. It was an emotional time and to make the change from work to retirement easier, we all went away for a holiday in Cornwall. My parents talked the proposed trip over with Jill, and they all agreed the change of environment would do me good, especially after the recent showdown with my Grandmother.

It was on our first day in Cornwall we saw Windrush.

Windrush was a beautiful bungalow, sitting on top of a hill just above the village of Coverack, overlooking the deep blue sea. The bungalow was situated in a peaceful cul-de-sac within two minutes walk from the beach. With a huge garden to keep my Dad happy, for him it was perfect.

Walking out of the garden gate you came to a small lane that twisted and turned down a steep hill, and led to a small fishing bay. The village had only a few shops but a large harbour. Coverack is a very scenic coastal village that, except for during high summer, was deserted all the time.

We were all admiring Windrush when suddenly we noticed the 'For Sale' sign.

"That's where were all going to live", said Dad with a huge smile.

Even before the row with Gran, Dad had decided long ago, as soon as he retired, he wanted to move away from Southend. Dad always wanted to get away from our Grandmother and he'd thought of moving to New Zealand years before but always lacked the courage to take Mum away from her Mother. They were always too enmeshed in one another' lives. Now it was urgent, before we all went mad, to move Mum and I away from Gran's clutches.

For Dad, living in Cornwall was his dream come true.

By the summer of 1990, my mental health had deteriorated considerably. I didn't go out, I had no friends and, outside of food, had no other interests. I had completely stopped talking to anyone and now lived in my own world of starvation. In place of a bubbly 22-year-old girl discovering her independence, I was now just a living shadow, like an unwanted piece of luggage dragged about by my parents.

I no longer had any say in the food I ate.

Even though all day, every day, I was starving, my thoughts were entirely controlled by the voice, which never allowed me to eat.

What the voice said, I did.

On our first night in Cornwall, we all stayed in a small hotel and it was the following morning at breakfast, Dad excitedly said he wanted to look at Windrush again. It was a drizzly and foggy day but that didn't deter my parents from arranging to meet the estate agent at three o'clock that afternoon. By now, I didn't want to see people at all, so while Mum and Dad looked round the bungalow, I stayed in the car alone. It was easier that way for me because I hated being asked questions about looking so thin and ill. By now I'd lost all self-confidence.

I was detached from absolutely everyone and by now had left my body and was no longer involved in normal life. It was as if I was now watching as an observer from the corner of the room, as everything happened to me. I so much wanted to reach out and rejoin the human race but the voice wouldn't let me. It had me imprisoned in my own anorexic shell. In my state, it made absolutely no difference to me where we lived. My parents, however, liked the bungalow and Dad made an acceptable offer. After the sale was agreed, they were both thrilled to bits and talked about nothing else for the whole week in Cornwall.

The following Sunday, we returned to Southend and put our own house on the market.

The one major stumbling block, of course, was Gran. Thinking she'd programmed Mum so well, my Grandmother didn't believe we would ever actually move. Gran was getting older. This was the time she would need my Mum the most and there was no way my Grandmother would ever accept the possibility that her own daughter would move 400 miles away. I felt guilty, thinking that perhaps my illness was one of the main reasons for us moving to Cornwall, but for the first time in my life, I felt valued. It seemed my parents were at last putting me before my Grandmother, saying my health was more important. Illness or no illness, at least Mum was getting away from Gran for the first time in her life.

My Grandmother's disbelief turned to shock as she saw the 'For Sale' notice up outside our house. That morning she stormed into the kitchen, the most furious look on her face, and literally spat out the words:
"So, you've gone and done it then."
My parents just looked at her in return. There was nothing for them to say.

We sold our house quite quickly and on the day we exchanged contracts, Mum realised she'd now have to tell Gran we were definitely leaving. Even with the 'For Sale' sign up outside the house, moving had become an unmentionable subject. In front of Gran it wasn't spoken about. I don't think even Mum had accepted we were actually moving, or if she did, the thought of looking Gran in the eye was too much for her. All the tranquillisers in the world were not going to help my Mother this time. She was having trouble adjusting to the idea that we were going to live 400 miles away from Gran.

Like the voice controlled me, Gran had always controlled Mum. They were still joined together by their invisible umbilical cord.

I was pleased to be leaving Southend, so relieved to get away from a town that held so many bad memories for me. Driving or walking down many of the streets evoked incredibly strong emotions, re-opening old wounds without warning. On top of that, I hated my Grandmother. I'd always been frightened of her and was so glad to move away as far as possible.

My brother Mark decided that he would stay in Southend for a while. His present job was based in the town but he had spoken with Dad about the possibility of finding a new job in Cornwall, so that he could join us in about a year's time.

Our moving date was originally set for November of 1990 but financial problems on the side of our buyers held up completion of the sale. November and December were very stressful months but just before Christmas, the phone call finally came through, saying completion could at last go ahead. Our moving date was set for January 29th and we all settled down to Christmas, feeling calmer than we had in a long time. There was still one huge problem left though. Gran. My Grandmother had to be told about our moving date but Mum found this impossible and just couldn't face doing it.

That Christmas my Grandmother was going to Ron's, so we were more or less guaranteed a few days peace. On Boxing Day, however, our festivities came to an abrupt end. Ron phoned to say he and Gran had a major argument after he'd told her about our move. Apparently over the Christmas dinner, she was boasting we weren't going to Cornwall after all. Before he could stop himself, he told her about the completion date set for January. Gran apparently dropped her knife and fork and went totally berserk, shouting at Ron. In the middle of her tirade, she suddenly fell to the floor, pretending her heart was weak. Lying on her back with her legs in the air, she insisted she would never survive such a shock. My Uncle had seen and heard all this pretence before. He was very annoyed and dragged Gran out to the car, taking her back home to Southend there and then.

On her return late that Christmas evening, Gran, totally oblivious to the row she'd recently had with Dad, and his orders not to come round again, stormed in and confronted Mum in the kitchen, shouting for hours.

"You're a weak person who couldn't even tell her own Mother about the house move. You had to get your brother to do all of your dirty work for you", she ranted on and on.

Mum was very upset and, leaving Gran on her own in the kitchen, ran up to my bedroom and asked me to speak with my Grandmother. Me speak? What was my Mother expecting? What a day that was. We had Gran running up and down the stairs and Mum crying in my bedroom. Dad was furious but as usual went to sleep, escaping again, while my brother Mark counted his fish. All the drama made no difference to our plans but simply emphasised how essential it was for us to move away.

That evening I really bore the brunt of my Grandmother's anger. Gran later found me hiding in my room. I was lying on my bed reading, when she walked in the door. Gran had me at a disadvantage from the start. I was flat on my back as she towered over me. At first I struggled to get up but she put a hand on my shoulder and held me down. I'll never forget her words.

"You do realise don't you Anna that even though you are moving away, I'll always be a part of your life? However far you run, I'll catch up with you. Remember, when you are feeling safe and smug in Cornwall, I'm nearer than you think."

With that, she turned on her heels and left my room, slamming the door behind her.

January 1991 was a very difficult month. Mum constantly worried about her Mother. My brother Mark was upset we were leaving and behaved strangely. We all worried about leaving Mark behind, and every day, he and Dad seemed to engage in the craziest rows about the right and wrong ways to pack.

I was very worried though about my own packing. Because I'd hidden so much food in my room, I was concerned some old mouldy chocolate or some other hidden food would now come to light and I wanted to pack by myself but doing it on my own however was unrealistic. I wasn't even strong enough to stand up properly any more, let alone pack. I had to have Dad's help. At this time it hurt me to walk. By now I had lost the use of my right leg.

While Dad worked his way through my wardrobe, I sat on the bed, carefully clearing out one drawer at a time. Luckily my Father didn't discover any food but I did. Under my jumpers were loads of old biscuits and chocolate bars.

Throughout the chaotic week of packing, I became weaker by the day. Finding it even more difficult to eat, I constantly cut back on food again which was easy now, with my parents totally preoccupied by their own worries. With all the moving going on, they weren't so vigilant about checking what I ate. I was allowed to prepare my own meals again, so I was free once more to cut down on calories.

Jill was far from pleased with everything that was going on. She was never happy that, in my state of health, we were moving to Cornwall but there was little she could do to stop it. Whereas once she'd argued so convincingly with Dr Lintell, saying I had M.E. not anorexia, my continued weight loss made it clear that Dr Lintell's diagnosis had been correct all along. There was no more to argue about and Jill, at this time, fully accepted I was definitely anorexic.

In recent weeks Jill, like my parents, had begun to see the obvious evidence of my appearance and was now panicking. She was totally at a loss to know what was the best thing to do. My condition was deteriorating rapidly and Jill, in a very serious voice, sat me down one morning and explained to me that now my weight had fallen so low, it had reached a critical level. My chances of recovering from anorexia were diminishing by the day. I think, deep down, at that stage Jill wanted to section me to a locked psychiatric hospital but now, with my parents moving four hundred miles away, visiting would be impossible. Regarding the situation as critical, she made Mum and Dad promise to make me see a new GP in Cornwall immediately we arrived and for this, she'd prepared a special report in advance, ready for the new doctor.

As the house sale completion date neared, my parents could clearly see that once again I was eating very little. However, this was a very stressful period and they didn't want to pressure me before the move. Instead, Mum and Dad decided to wait until we were settled in Cornwall before talking with me once again about my diet. For us as a family, nothing else mattered at this time, apart from moving as far away from my Grandmother as possible.

Finally it was time to go. The removers arrived on the afternoon of January 28th and packed everything except for our beds, which they were returning for early the following morning.

That afternoon, it felt so strange watching my bedroom furniture being carried out the front door into the van. It was 3.30 in the afternoon and the children were leaving school for the day. Little did they know that in this cupboard and chest of drawers, I had hidden hundreds of biscuits and chocolate bars over all those years.

Not wanting to accept the seriousness of my illness, we were all burying our heads in the sand in thinking that going to Cornwall was going to be the answer to all our problems. Both my parents and I were putting all our hopes into the move. We believed the moment we walked through the door at Windrush, I would be magically cured.

The anorexic brain is very complex. I had starved myself for years. My weight was now at a critical level but in my confused subconscious mind, I believed as soon as we set foot in Cornwall, I would eat normally. I was certain that, once there, I could switch off both the voice and my fear of food.

Mum and Dad had by now adopted quite different ideas about how to help me deal with the anorexia. Dad was all for keeping me at home, convinced that living by the sea, he and Mum could gently nurse me back to health. He was certain all I needed was tender loving care. Dad was right, but that tender loving care was coming twenty years too late. Mum outwardly agreed with him but privately had other definite ideas. She didn't want the responsibility and thought I should go immediately into hospital.

Finally, with everything packed and the old house totally empty, it was time to go. Together with Mum and Dad, we stood in the empty home and all cried. I don't remember much about the journey down to Cornwall, except for the meal we had in a service station. We were all waiting in line together but, when my parents asked me to choose a meal, I totally flipped out. A queue was forming behind us and Dad, seeing my distress, told my Mother to take me to an empty table while he chose some food for me. I felt so stupid, such a failure - now unable to even make the most simple decisions any more.

We finally arrived at Windrush in the darkness of early evening and, entering through the garage door leading into the kitchen, were met by our new neighbours waiting to surprise and welcome us with cups of coffee. The sight of those people scared me stiff. I was so frightened, I couldn't even say hello properly and, without a word, ran into the bedroom. Dad came in after me and sat on the floor beside me, trying to calm me down.

A short while later, the removal van arrived, but I was in such a state I just couldn't get up. I just sat there transfixed, with everyone moving furniture around me. For the next two hours I just stayed on the floor. Much later, when the removal men finally left at about nine o'clock, Mum made us a light snack. By now we were all totally exhausted and went to bed in rooms filled with huge cardboard boxes.

Both me and the voice settled in quickly together in our new home. Our new bungalow was much larger than the house we had just left, and we both could disappear without being noticed. The first thing the voice and I did in our new home was to start hiding food. It was so easy for us, once the voice had spotted the difference in our seating arrangements in the lounge. It was to be used to our advantage.

"Anna, look. Your parents can't see what you're doing. Hide food now."

I could now quite easily slip food into a napkin and dispose of it later.

The voice now completely controlled me.

I was addicted to starving myself and to break this addiction, I would have had to face the thought of sitting down to regular meals, like everyone else. There was no way I could contemplate this absurd idea. The anorexia had taken over and the voice was in charge.

I was terrified now.

In the peace and quiet of Cornwall, what terrified me most was the voice.

Somehow I'd always believed that ultimately I was in control. I was anorexic but deep down, I still decided how little food I ate and how much weight I wanted to lose.

But now I, Anna, had no say in the matter.

The voice was in total control and didn't want me to eat anything at all.

It was around this time, the voice decided we should destroy ourselves completely.

"We must stop eating now and get thinner than ever before. Thin is nice. Thin is beautiful."

I was so frightened. I knew now the voice was going to kill me. Soon I would be dead.

I wanted to cry out and tell Mum and Dad about the voice but every time I tried to speak, the voice told me to shut up.

"Just talk to me", the voice commanded.

The only conversations I had now were with the voice and what the voice said, I did. I was enslaved.

Anorexia had taken me over completely.

WINDRUSH – THE ISOLATED
BUNGALOW BY THE SEA

GETTING THINNER

Chapter 10

THE GRANDMOTHER STRIKES BACK

We hadn't been living in Windrush long before we had our first nightmare experience. Early one morning, I looked out the window to see a huge removal van parked across the road. I called my Father who came to look.
"Oh my God, no! Not again", he sighed.

When I was young, Gran had followed us across town after our first move. A month after Mum and Dad originally moved into their new house on the opposite side of town to Gran, they'd looked out of the window to see a removal van with men carrying all my Grandmother's belongings into the house opposite.

Now the same thing was happening all over again.

None of us could believe our eyes. I rushed into the garden and peering over the hedge. I gasped in horror. Here was my Grandmother, walking from the house to the van. I wanted to run away. This couldn't be true. Gran really had moved to Cornwall.

Dad was furious and ran across the road, ready for battle.
"I'm going to sort this out, once and for all", he said.

Twenty minutes later, my Father returned with a huge grin all over his face.
"She's one of the sweetest old ladies I've ever met", he said. "Though a little potty. She tried to put salt instead of

sugar in my coffee." Turning to me, he said "She looks like your Gran but that's all they have in common." We all sighed with relief. Although we'd moved 400 miles away, we were still all prisoners of my Grandmother.

We'd only just got over the shock when early one morning, a few days later, there was a ring at the bell. Dad opened the door. This time there was no mistaking that familiar figure. Standing there with a large suitcase was my Grandmother. Dad took one look, then before anyone could catch their breath, he escorted her down the drive shouting:
"I'll take you to a hotel. There's no way you are sleeping here. No way."
Mum and I just watched speechless. This was all so out of character for Dad. My Father put her suitcase in the boot and practically threw Gran in the car.

Dad returned an hour later, telling us my Grandmother was now booked into a hotel in the village.

"I can't stop her visiting Cornwall but she's not staying here", he said with a huge grin.

Dad looked so proud of himself that day. For only the second time in twenty-five years, he'd risen to the occasion and confronted my Grandmother.

The following morning, Mum rang Gran and after many arguments with Dad, who didn't want her round at all any more, it was finally agreed she could visit our bungalow but strictly only for a few hours.

I didn't know what to wear on the day my Grandmother visited. For years she'd always criticised my clothes, my size and everything about me. I tried on my favourite jeans but in them I looked so fat. I looked at my bottom and legs in the mirror and saw a huge body. Like all anorexics, my view of myself was completely distorted. I just couldn't see the severe emaciation, the terrible state I was actually in. My bottom and legs had completely disappeared, all that was left was skin and bone. I now weighed under 6 stones (under 84lbs.) but sadly, in my eyes, those days I still believed I was extremely fat.

Mum met Gran at the village bus stop and together they walked back to the bungalow. Dad and I waited reluctantly for her to arrive and, hearing my Grandmother's voice, I started to shake. I couldn't bear to be anywhere near this woman. She was horrible and hated us having anything nice. Her method of mentally coping with Mum and Dad moving to a new bungalow was to imagine it as a tiny, scruffy, derelict place. The reality of seeing Windrush, a lovely spacious new home, made her hopping mad.

Pompously she strode through our house, making snide remarks about every room. In an effort to quieten her down, Mum suggested coffee and cakes. Gran immediately followed Mum into the kitchen to help. While everything was being prepared, I could hear my Grandmother talking about me in a voice so loud it was obvious I was supposed to hear.

"What has happened to Anna? She looks absolutely appalling. I thought she looked bad enough a few months ago. Now she looks positively repulsive", Gran continued.

Sitting in the lounge, hearing that so familiar voice, I cringed, unable to bring myself to look at Dad. My parents who, deep down, were still totally controlled by my Grandmother, said absolutely nothing to defend me from this woman's latest outburst.

Mum and Gran joined us with plates of cakes and mugs of coffee.

"Take one", Gran hissed, putting the cakes under my nose.

I took the smallest one and picked at it, one crumb at a time. I felt so intimidated being so near to that woman. I wanted to cry. Mum and Dad had faithfully promised me I would never have to have tea with Gran again, yet once more here we were all together playing happy families. I felt betrayed. I couldn't calm down, but then the voice rescued me with soothing calorific poetry.

"Bread", I thought. "80 calories a slice. Cheese 114 calories per ounce. Butter 594 calories per 100 grammes."

It was okay - the voice was back in charge. I felt safe. I felt better. I looked up to find Gran staring at me. The look took me back to my childhood days, locked up in her bungalow.

My Grandmother stayed for about an hour. Watching her, my mind was locked into the prison of my childhood when suddenly, without a word or backward glance, Gran stood up and walked out of the door.

Chapter 11

TROUBLE IN THE SEWERS

My life was deteriorating around me, growing worse by the day. With the voice demanding I dropped more and more food items from my diet, my calorie intake soon fell below 500 a day.

"Throw more food away", the voice continually repeated.

When I looked in the mirror all I could see were huge lumps of rippling fat, engulfing my body. The anorexic illness in my mind couldn't see that I was now so dangerously thin that my ribs were individually visible.

Hiding food now became my chief obsession.

It wasn't long though before I got caught again and all hell broke loose. The bathroom and toilet at Windrush were separate and my parents were having an additional new toilet plumbed into the bathroom. In early March 1991 the conversions started.

This meant that both bathrooms were out of action for long periods of time during the day. I didn't dare risk flushing food while the plumber was working in case he saw me, so I saved it all up and flushed it in one go each night after the workmen had left.

One Sunday at the end of March, a couple of weeks after the plumber had finished, my world totally collapsed. I was having a bath when suddenly I could hear Dad's voice shouting to Mum outside the door. He was going mad. All I heard were the words:

"I can't believe it! She's really done it this time! This is the final straw! I just don't want to call her my daughter any longer!"

I looked out of the window and could see Dad by one of the manholes. There was water everywhere and I knew immediately that all the food I'd flushed away for so many weeks, had now completely blocked the entire drainage system. I found Mum in her bedroom.

"Is Dad angry with me?" I asked her.

"Angry?" she sharply replied. "We're both angry with you. We've had enough! You've pushed your Father too far this time. I don't know if he'll ever forgive you for what you've done and to be honest I don't blame him!"

My legs gave way from under me and, bursting into tears, I collapsed in a heap on the floor. I didn't know to what extent I'd blocked the drains but I knew, from my Father's outburst, I'd done something very bad.

Mum kept snapping and told me the whole story. Dad had discovered water rising from under a manhole. My Father found the drains completely blocked with all the food I'd thrown away. Too embarrassed to explain what had happened, there was no way he was going to call in a specialist firm to clear the blockage. He had to do it. Dad was now trying to clear away all the wrapped parcels of biscuits, bread, cakes and potatoes that I'd disposed of and at that moment, wasn't having much success. Mum ordered me to my room and told me to keep out of Dad's way. By now my Father was really furious and the last person he wanted to see was me.

It took Dad several hours to clear the drains and all the time I could hear him muttering to himself:
"That's it! I've had enough of that girl!"

Eventually Dad finished and came storming into my bedroom.

"Well that was a good start to a new life! I presume this was your way of helping us to settle into our new home! Look at my hands! Do you realise what you've just made me do? That was the most disgusting job I've ever had to do and it was all your fault! I hope you're proud of yourself! If I were you, I'd stay well out of my sight for a few days!"

"Dad please forgive me, I'll never throw food away again. Please don't be angry with me."

Hysterically, I continued begging my Dad for forgiveness but he just walked away, closing my bedroom door behind him. In the silence of my room, I felt my lifelong loneliness.

The atmosphere over the next few days was horrible, with my parents completely ignoring me as if I wasn't even there.

Not that this made much difference because for twenty-two years it had never felt as though I was there anyway.

Chapter 12

A WEIGHT ON MY MIND

On the following Monday morning, Jill, my old psychiatric nurse, rang and was very annoyed. She was furious with my parents and wanted to know why she still hadn't heard from the local health clinic. Jill gave Mum and Dad an immediate ultimatum. Now really concerned, she told my parents if they didn't do something that morning, she would be forced to intervene, even from 400 miles away. Several phone calls later, an official appointment was made for the following day at the local medical centre.

I panicked. This was the end.

I hadn't been weighed now by a doctor for months. My weight had dropped steadily and I knew there would be trouble once the new low weight was found out. Back in Southend, I'd become complacent about Dr Lee and his mild threats of hospitalisation every time my weight went down. Up until now, I'd always got away with it but now I was going to meet a new doctor, and at my weight, there was every chance I'd be forced immediately into hospital.

I had to find a way to cheat the system, to fool the doctor into thinking I was heavier than I really was.

The voice came up with the immediate answer.

"Make yourself heavier. Hide garden stones in your clothes!" the voice said, defiantly.

Over the next two days, every time I went into the garden, I collected some small pebbles. Just a couple at a time so that I didn't draw attention to myself. Each night, once Mum and Dad were safely in bed, I began sewing these stones into the lining of my jacket. It was a lightweight jacket and I was certain they'd let me wear it while I was weighed. I soon collected enough stones to make the jacket 10 lbs. heavier.

The night before the appointment I couldn't sleep at all. My mind was filled with thoughts of running away but where would I run to in the middle of nowhere in Cornwall? I had little choice but to attend the doctor's appointment.

The following morning, we all drove to the local health clinic. I was certain they'd admit me to the local hospital on the spot and start force-feeding me. We sat in the waiting room, with me staring at the floor. Eventually a nurse came out, calling Mum and Dad in, asking me to wait. I wasn't alone though in that waiting room. The voice was with me.

"Don't tell them anything", the voice quietly whispered

It seemed like an eternity before Dad re-appeared about five minutes later, telling me it was my turn. By this time I was shaking and could feel the sweat running down the inside of my arms. The nurse greeted me with a warm smile, asking me to remove my shoes.

It was time to be weighed.

I took my shoes off, nervously holding onto my jacket as I wrapped it tightly round my body. First the nurse measured me and then asked me to hop on the scales. I started to giggle. I couldn't understand what was happening to me. Here I was, at one of the most frightening times of my life, and I was giggling. All I could think of were the nurse's words:
"Hop on the scales."
Why was I asked to hop? Would I be lighter if I only stood on one leg? I laughed. It was just so bizarre.

Reality came rushing back as I heard the nurse's words.
"You are quite light for your height aren't you?"
Immediately I jumped back defensively, telling her:
"Oh no. I've just got a very fast metabolism."
The nurse seemed to accept this information; after all she was quite thin herself.

I looked at the clock. The time was ticking away. Three minutes had already passed.
"Surely the medical must almost be over", I prayed.

I had just started to feel slightly calmer, when I heard the dreaded words.
"Would you mind taking your jacket off for a minute please Anna?"
Taking your jacket off, the words spun round, repeating in my head. I looked at the nurse in horror.

"Don't worry", she said. "I'm not going to do anything nasty to you. I just need to take your blood pressure, it's a painless procedure."
I was trapped.

Set point.

If I said no, the nurse would want to know why I wouldn't remove my jacket. If I took off the jacket, she would see how thin I was.

Match point.

Walking towards me, she said:
"Here, let me help you", as she reached for my jacket.
"No", I shouted. "I'll do it."
I couldn't let her touch my coat; she'd immediately feel how heavy it was. I slipped it from my shoulders, making sure the pebbles didn't knock together.

"Roll up your sleeve", the nurse said.
We had finally reached the moment of truth. I rolled up my sleeve and heard a sharp intake of breath.

Game over.

The nurse was totally shocked, looking at my arm, just skin and bone. Here was an arm, covered in scars from years of self-harming. My arm was so thin with the bones poking through. Quietly, the nurse sat down beside me.
"It's all right, don't be frightened. I'm not here to hurt you but I need you to stand on the scales again."
She put her arm around me, saying:
"Here, hand me your jacket. Don't be afraid Anna."

I had no choice. I gave the nurse my coat full of stones. She must have felt the heaviness but said nothing. Neither did she remark when my weight registered nearly a stone less than previously. The nurse didn't say a word; she just looked me in the eyes and smiled. She took my blood pressure and, handing me back my jacket, said:
"It'll be all right. We'll help you. I'll just be a minute or two", she said, leaving the room.
The nurse returned with an older doctor, who thoroughly examined me.

The doctor told me to sit down and, strangely enough, although tormented, I felt a wave of relief come over me. My anorexia had been discovered at last and momentarily, the voice had been silenced. In front of me, the doctor phoned someone and made an appointment. His words were quite decisive.
"We have a severe case of anorexia. She should be admitted immediately. She needs emergency treatment."

"Anna", he said, turning to me. "Tomorrow you will have a visitor coming to see you at home at 3.00 pm."
"Who?" I asked.
"The Head Psychiatrist from Trengweath Hospital."

Mum and Dad didn't say a word driving home. It wasn't necessary, it had all been said so many times before. That night our house was like a morgue. Absolutely no spoken words. I was weak and laid on the couch all evening, and every time my parents passed me, they just stared in silence. Their eyes said it all.

I was in despair.

Chapter 13

THEY ARE COMING TO TAKE ME AWAY

The following morning, the doctor I'd seen the day before, rang Dad and told him to collect some rehydration drinks to sustain me until the psychiatrist came in the afternoon. It was while Dad was away that my Mother spoke with me.

I talked with Mum about my appointment with Dr Parkinson, asking her if she thought the doctors would take me into hospital. Encouragingly, she didn't think that would happen. I asked her if she was going to bring the subject up but she promised she wouldn't. Emphatically, she reassured me she would definitely tell them not to take me into hospital.

About an hour later, Dad returned with the rehydration drink. I tried desperately to drink it but I couldn't. It was fizzy and I couldn't swallow more than a few mouthfuls. I was always unable to drink fizzy drinks. My parents thought I was, as usual, just being difficult over eating and drinking and I could see the exasperation in their faces. Ironically, this time however, I wasn't worried about the calories. As much as I wanted to, I really couldn't physically swallow this liquid. I tried to take small sips but it was impossible and eventually we all just gave up.

The whole day seemed unreal. I glanced up at the clock, it was well into the afternoon. Time was ticking away.

My appointment with the psychiatrist was set for three o'clock.

I knew the end was near.

Anorexia nervosa had won.

I could hear the voice laughing out loud.

"Well done Anna, you did as you were told."

"Anna, you've been a good girl."

At precisely three, a big blue car pulled up on our drive and I was shocked when I saw two women getting out. I had expected only one male doctor. The bell rang and I felt physically sick. Mum answered the door, showing Dr Black and Dr Margaret to the lounge. She went into the kitchen to make some drinks, leaving me with the two doctors. They looked quite serious as one began speaking. One of the women explained Dr Parkinson, the chief consultant, was in Australia for a holiday but they were his senior house officers based at Trengweath Hospital. Both women were quite young really, only about ten years older than me. They started by generally chatting with me about normal, everyday things. The doctors weren't asking me any questions about my eating habits or behaviour around food. I was surprised but certainly wasn't lulled into a false sense of security. Biding my time, I waited for the onslaught to start.

My Mother returned with the coffee and began pleading with them to take me into hospital. Ten minutes earlier,

Mum had said she would not let them put me in hospital but now she wanted them to. I was devastated. My Mum had now turned into my final betrayer.

After all she'd told me that morning, I really couldn't believe what I was hearing. My Mother knew how desperately afraid I was of going to hospital but here she was actually asking them outright to take me away that day.

Dad just sat in the corner as usual, silent.

All control was now being taken out of my hands. I was no longer allowed to make decisions for myself. Other people were deciding what was best for me.
"I don't want to go to Trengweath, I want to stay at home", I kept saying but nobody was paying any attention to me.
They were all just talking amongst themselves.

After an hour, the senior of the two doctors turned to me and said:
"Anna, we are taking you into hospital today. You are not strong enough to cope with this illness alone."
I was desolate. My worst nightmare had come true and I was now too weak to argue.

The doctors had no choice. They could see an extremely sick girl, obviously emaciated.

A girl with a waxy white complexion.

A girl whose hands were tinged blue from the cold.

A girl who hadn't eaten properly for months.

A girl whose weight was now dangerously low at six stones (84 lbs.).

They knew there was only one safe place for this girl. A hospital, where she could be monitored and cared for, until her weight returned to a safe level.

I began begging them.

"Just give me anything to eat," I cried. "Anything, I'll eat anything. Please I beg you."

I got on my knees saying, "Let me stay at home please."

To this, my Mother curtly replied:
"You couldn't even hold down the rehydration drink. Could she Mike?"
"No darling", replied my Father with his usual blank look.
"We can't cope with her any longer", my Mother now continued, addressing the doctors.
I felt completely betrayed.

Now the voice was shouting loudly in my head.

"How much proof do you need? I told you your Mother hated you, didn't I? They will never let you out of hospital until you are this blobby lump of fat. All the hard slimming work you've done will disappear."

One of the doctors phoned Trengweath Hospital and confirmed there was a vacant bed. They asked my parents to pack a suitcase as quickly as possible and drive me to hospital then and there. Somehow in the past I'd always been able to convince the doctors that I wasn't really sick. Why wouldn't these two understand?

Hospital stays are lengthy for anorexics. Gaining weight is not a speedy process, it can take months. My logical mind knew I was at least 3½ stones (49 lbs.) below the expected weight for my height. I really didn't think that once they had me in there, I'd ever leave the hospital again.

As soon as the doctors left, Dad hugged me and cried his eyes out. My Mother however, sat down and went into a lengthy speech assuring us both that she was just as upset as we were but wouldn't cry because somebody had to be strong. Mum's speech sounded cold, like a newscaster. My Dad however was overcome, saying:
"If only I'd known you were ill. I didn't realise. It'll be okay, sweetheart, honest it will. I don't want you to go into hospital. It'll just be for a while and your Mum and I will visit you daily. Your body's giving up. Please let them help you. For my sake, please."

"For his sake?" I thought.

Once again he'd said the magic words "For our sakes" which, as always, worked like in the past and made me do as he said. All my life I'd always done everything for their sakes.

Typical of my Father's character, I don't think, up until this time, he was even able to admit how ill I was. He had always buried his head in the sand, trying to pretend nothing was really happening, but now there was no running away from the fact that I had anorexia. Dad was clearly upset, losing his only daughter to an illness with no logic.

Throughout all the trauma of my life, I had coped but now it was different. Never before was I so desperate. I was familiar with the abuse. I knew it from a child but now I was entering the complete unknown. I was going to encounter strange people I didn't know, on a ward in a psychiatric hospital. I was frightened, very frightened. What would they feed me? What tests would they carry out?

Was I being abandoned for good?

An hour or so later my case was packed and we were all ready to leave. Moving to Cornwall was supposed to be the start of our new life but as usual, I'd failed again and screwed it all up. If only I'd been able to eat, I wouldn't be going into hospital now. I was no safer in our new home than I had been in Southend. My Grandmother was still inside my head, her voice systematically destroying me. All the powerful messages she fed into me as a child, were now killing me.

Finally at about 6.00 pm, with Mum and Dad, I left Windrush and drove off to the hospital. As I got in the car I began to wonder if I was I leaving for good. Watching the village of Coverack disappear felt like the end for me. Throughout the journey, nobody spoke a word and before I realised it, we were outside Trengweath Hospital.

It was a big building, and after three wrong turnings, we finally found the entrance gates tucked beside a small bridge. As we entered the grounds, I could physically sense my freedom vanishing. I was losing control and I couldn't do anything now to stop the train of events.

It was dark as we arrived and the building seemed hugely imposing. Trengweath was a psychiatric hospital, catering for all aspects of mental health. It was a crumbling building in the middle of a town that was dying, as its tin mining industry had slowly collapsed. Patients were admitted suffering with anything from drug and alcohol addiction, depression and schizophrenia to eating disorders.

My parents and I walked around the building three times before, finally, one of the catering staff pointed out the way to reception. We were in the middle of a heavy storm and crying, my tears merged with the drops of rain.

As we entered the main doors we were stopped by an official looking man. Members of staff guarded the entrance at all times, to prevent any patient leaving unsupervised. I felt trapped. This wasn't a hospital I was being admitted to. It was more like a prison. I was being incarcerated and it felt, for me, there was absolutely no way out.

A nurse called Chris, who had been waiting specially for me to arrive, greeted us at the reception. She took the three of us into a side room, then together with her colleague, another nurse called Rachel, started the long process of admission. Chris and Rachel were both young nurses in their mid-'20s.

The registration period was a belittling experience for me. I was a human reject, being discussed like I was about to be exhibited in some glass showcase. So many forms to be filled in and signed. It all felt so permanent to me. I desperately wanted to run away but I couldn't move. Mum stayed relatively calm but Dad was clearly upset and struggled to speak. Mum, as usual, did most of the talking.

The admission forms took about three-quarters of an hour to complete, then Chris and Rachel took me to my room. At that time, there were no other anorexic patients in the hospital so it was decided to place me in a small side room with Cath, a young mother suffering badly with post-natal depression. She apparently had tried to commit suicide and was being observed under different medications to try to alleviate her symptoms.

The room was pleasant, with two beds separated by thin wooden partitions, making them into individual little cubicles. In comparison to a huge hospital ward, the surroundings were really quite comfortable.

By this time, Dad just couldn't cope any longer. After he and Mum saw the room he suddenly became very emotional and, with tears in his eyes, announced they were leaving. That night I hugged my Father, as I've never hugged anyone before. I wanted Dad to tell the nursing staff this was all a big mistake that he was going to take me home with him. I tried to hug Mum too, but it just didn't feel the same. Moments later I watched, traumatised, as my parents walked from my room. Now totally alone, I cried and cried, looking out through the window. My room overlooked a railway viaduct, which I found out later, many people had committed suicide by jumping off. At that very moment, I wanted to do exactly that.

Ten minutes passed, before the nurses Chris and Rachel re-appeared. They both hugged me endlessly, then checked through my belongings, cataloguing absolutely everything. They removed objects they thought potentially dangerous, such as razors or scissors. Every item I'd brought was written down on another form and I was handed the sheet to sign. Again I felt humiliated, as this inventory was carried out on me.

Both nurses left for some time after this, then returned to book me in for my full admission medical. Every new patient being admitted has a head-to-toe examination in case of other undetected illnesses that need treating.

During this period, Cath, the other patient, returned to the room. She smiled at me and I tried to smile back. Her smile though was anything but bright.

"Hello", she said. "My name's Cath but then I expect you already know don't you? And I know you're Anna, they've already put your name sticker up on the door. You're obviously not staying just overnight are you? They only ever put name tags up on the door if they think you're going to be here for a long time."

Her words depressed me even more. She continued.

"I can guess what you're in here for; you're anorexic aren't you? I've got postnatal depression. I can't bear to be near my baby. I tried to kill myself. They want me to go and see my baby soon. I'm really frightened, I only want my son, I don't want my daughter at all."

I was very withdrawn and didn't reply much. It was an amazing first conversation to have with anyone. Really quite bizarre. Soon, however, I was to get used to this way of everyday hospital chatter.

Suddenly Cath, for no reason, became very agitated and without saying another word, just got up and walked out the room. I wasn't supposed to get out of bed but, feeling very nervous myself, I got up and walked down the hall. It was changeover time and the new set of nurses starting their shift were being briefed. Next to the nurses station were two rooms with just glass window panels on the door. I was horrified to see a completely bare room with just a mattress in the corner. It reminded me of looking into a cage of animals in the zoo. A man was sitting in what looked like a straitjacket. He started screaming and began hitting his head on the wall. There was blood dripping from his ear. Suddenly he saw me and stopped. Coming over to the bars, he stared at me, saying:
"Help me! Help me!"
I wanted to run away but my legs gave way and I fell on the floor. A nurse came by and put me in a wheelchair and took me to my room.

A few minutes later my own nurse, Chris, returned. She had heard what had happened but instead of being annoyed, just made me promise not to get out of bed again.
"Anyhow you're getting out of bed now. Its time for your admission medical, I'm taking you downstairs", Chris smiled reassuringly.

She lifted me back into the wheelchair and took me down to the examination room.

I was wheeled into the clinic to find Dr Margaret waiting for me. Earlier in the day I was extremely hostile towards this doctor but now at least she was someone I already knew which, in a strange hospital, was most reassuring.

The doctor weighed me and yet, even in clothes, I barely made it to six stones (84 lbs.). She then completed a very complicated full medical and tested just about every part of my body. It was about ten o'clock by the time Dr Margaret finished the examination, and though she urgently wanted an ECG trace taken of my heart and various blood tests, she said all that would have to wait until the morning, as there just weren't enough staff available at that time of night.

It was getting late and by this time I'd become very agitated and, quite hysterically, began begging Dr Margaret for a specific release date to work towards. I had to know when I was going home. For me, having just been admitted, an open-ended stay was too overwhelming.
"When will I get out of here?" I kept on and on at Dr Margaret.

Dr Margaret tried to calm me down but confessed she just didn't know how long I would have to stay. They wanted me in hospital to stabilise my condition physically, as well as mentally.
"Calm down, we'll get you well", she said.

She went on to explain my weight was at a critical level for my height and I needed to put on at least a few pounds before I'd be allowed off bed rest - it was truly a serious situation. With a very stern look, she told me I could die from a heart attack at any moment.

"Your health is far worse than you think."

Hearing this, I was badly shocked. I hadn't realised I was so ill.

When Dr Margaret had finished all the tests, I was wheeled back to my room and put back to bed with strict instructions not to move. Chris tucked me in, saying she would leave me for a while. She was going to the nurses station to write up my end of day reports.

Some considerable time later, Chris returned to my room. She apologised for leaving me alone for so long but said there had been an emergency situation with one of the patients. I had suspected there had been some kind of problem. I could hear the screams and cries very clearly from my room.

Chris made me some Horlicks, then sat with me while I tried to drink it. After I'd finished, she asked me if I was okay to go to sleep. She introduced me to the night nurses, explaining I only had to push my buzzer and they would come.

"Here, let me give you a hug", Chris said, putting her arms round me.

With Chris holding me, I cried, as the years of hurt and feelings of being alone flooded out.

My Grandmother had done a good job.

I was a very confused person who couldn't understand why Chris was hugging me. Why wasn't she shouting at me?

When Chris left my room, I just turned into my pillow and wept silently for hours. The Redruth Town Hall Clock chimed every quarter of an hour and that first night, I heard every single chime, from midnight to six the following morning. I have not felt so alone before or since.

Awake all night, I saw the dawn break that morning in late April 1991.

Chapter 14

TRENGWEATH HOSPITAL

Eventually, with it already daylight, I drifted off to sleep for about half an hour, waking to find a nurse standing over me with a glass of milk. The night nurse explained that as soon as the day shift arrived, someone would be along to discuss what I was eating for breakfast. The day nurses would also give me a bath.

Dr Margaret had left strict orders that I wasn't permitted to walk anywhere. The doctors were afraid I'd faint or fall over. There was also the risk of a heart attack.

Rachel appeared at about 8.00 am, giving me a hug.
"Don't worry, we'll take everything really slowly here. We won't force any food on you. You just eat whatever you can and relax", she said. "Now, shall I go and get you some breakfast?" she smiled. "What do you feel you could manage? A piece of toast? A small amount of cereal?"
My mind, like all anorexics', went into panic mode merely over the prospect of eating.

Calculating the calories, I decided on the cereal anyhow. I wasn't sure how much butter they would put on the toast or how many slices they would give me. The cereal seemed a safer bet. Surely they couldn't fit that much in a bowl I thought to myself.

Waiting for the breakfast to arrive was so strange, having spent the last five years constantly on a diet. I didn't know how food tasted any more. Amidst all the terror of being in this institution, there was also a weird feeling of safety, like a young child feels when he is fed in a high chair. Now, in hospital, I was being forced to eat. This was a relief because, like all anorexics, I had always felt hungry. For years, day and night, I desperately wanted to eat. It was only the voice that stopped me eating, even though my whole adult life I was starving. The voice had for years been a central point of my life, and the only way to get the voice to love me was not to eat. Now, with the nurses threatening me with a drip feed, the voice was overruled and had no choice but to allow me the food being given by the hospital.

At last I could eat.

Ten minutes later, Rachel returned with a bowl filled to the brim with Rice Krispies and milk. Looking at that bowl of cereal, I was filled with panic at the amount of food I was expected to eat.

She sat beside me on a stool.
"I'll stay with you while you eat", she said. "There will always be someone with you at meal times from now on because we are all concerned about your physical health."
A huge wave of relief came over me because with the nurses present, the voice was losing its control. She told me they would be very careful how much food they gave me each time, because if the amount was excessive, my stomach could burst.

Slowly I began to eat the soggy cereal, each spoonful consisting of only one or two tiny bubbles of rice. I felt guilty keeping Rachel from seeing other patients, but couldn't force the food down any faster. I kept apologising for my slowness but Rachel wasn't concerned.

"Don't hurry", she said. "I am assigned only to you all day today. We will take things as slowly as you need to take them."

It took me nearly an hour to eat that small bowl of Rice Krispies. When I eventually finished, I wanted to laugh as Rachel offered me toast, but she accepted my refusal with a smile. Soon after, Rachel bathed me, then put me back in bed to wait for Dr Margaret.

Waiting for the doctor, I drifted off into a vivid dream. Half asleep, half awake, a film replay of my life started to visibly show inside my mind. I was alone in a huge cinema, watching myself on a big screen. An usherette came round selling ice creams.

"Are you mad?" I said. "I'm Anna. I never eat fatty ice creams."

She left as the movie began. The opening scene was me - eight years old, alone in Hamleys, petrified, looking for my Grandmother. I could see Gran shouting, as the image switched to a plate of fish with big bones, surrounded by mountains of mashed potatoes.

"Eat it! Eat it!" Gran was screaming, hitting me on the leg.

I tried to wake up to escape from my dream but the camera switched to my Grandmother's bathroom. She was washing me, saying:

"Fat children grow up to be fat adults!"

The scene faded, reopening in a busy clothes store, again with someone shouting:

"You and your skinny legs!"

It was Emma from College. The dream continued now, with the camera showing me diving into the school swimming pool. As I surfaced, there was my Grandmother standing by the pool, holding a huge plate of cakes. I tried to swim away but she was throwing the cakes at me in the water. Reaching to pull myself out of the water, I found Gran pulling me by my hand.

"You were having a nightmare. Calm down, everything is all right."

I opened my eyes and there was Dr Margaret, holding my hand, sitting on my bed.

I talked with the doctor for about an hour. She was trying to explore the psychological reasons behind my eating disorder. The doctor explained we needed to look into my past, to investigate the origins of my anorexic thoughts.

"Your anorexic behaviour started when you were young, we must find out where", she said, with a friendly smile. As we chatted, a glimmer of light appeared when, for the first time, I could see myself clearly now as an innocent child being tormented by my Grandmother. At last I was beginning to understand the hurt and confusion in that child. Momentarily it was all beginning to make sense, when my thoughts were suddenly interrupted. The radiologist had arrived, pushing a portable Electrocardiogram machine. It was time for my ECG (a test on my heartbeat). She attempted to attach the electrodes to my chest, but because I had lost so much weight, it was futile. My body now was reduced to bone, with no flesh to stick the electrodes to. Eventually, with

"What will my 'target weight' be?" I queried.

"I don't like working to a set target weight", Dr Ken replied. "The figure that we set for you will be the lowest weight it is safe for you to walk around at without risking a heart attack or multiple organ failure. We'll discuss everything tomorrow, when I've had a chance to look at your charts and the results of your tests." Pulling himself to his feet he jokingly said, "I really am getting far too old for this crawling about on the floor lark."

He gave my hand one last squeeze, saying:

"Look after yourself little one. I'll be back tomorrow. Don't worry, we'll take care of you now."

Visiting hours at Trengweath were 3.00 pm to 5.30 pm. My parents arrived that first day on the dot of 3.00 o'clock, armed with flowers and cards to brighten my room, staying until 5.30. We didn't speak much. Both Mum and Dad were lost for words and really I was glad of the silence.

Shortly after my parents had left, Chris, my other nurse, came back with my tea. It was sandwiches again. This time there was also a dessert on my tray and, seeing it, I panicked. I kept staring at the small pot of cheesecake. The nurse noticed my anxiety and tried to calm me by moving the cake from my line of vision.

The sandwiches this time were egg mayonnaise. Once again, I marvelled at the amazing taste I was experiencing. It was now six or seven years since I'd eaten certain foods like egg or cheese, and I'd completely forgotten what they were like. Now those eggs tasted so wonderful. It took nearly one hour for me to eat two of the sandwich quarters. Chris looked at me and said:

"We don't want to push you too fast Anna, but if you eat one mouthful more than lunch time, I can write it down on your chart."

Chart? What Chart?

This was the first time I'd heard of 'The Chart'. What was this Chart? Where was it kept? Who saw it? Apparently, a record of everything that I ate and drank on a daily basis was observed. Every single mouthful I consumed was recorded.

I managed two extra bites of the third quarter plus one spoonful of cheesecake when, from nowhere, the voice began screaming:

"Fat children grow up to be fat adults!"

I began crying uncontrollably. Chris put down the tray, reached over, and just hugged me. She held me, gently stroking me, telling me everything would be all right.

Chris stayed with me for several hours. Later that day I was given the first of many Build-Up Drinks, which tasted like a strawberry milkshake. These drinks are special meal replacements, which meant weight gain, and immediately I started to panic again. Mentally, I just couldn't cope knowing that thousands of extra calories were going into me each day, even if I ate nothing.
"Must I have these drinks often?" I asked.
"Not too often", Chris replied. "The doctor has only written you down for three a day."

What was I hearing? Three a day meant I would be drinking in excess of 1,000 calories each day before any of the food I was eating. I began to argue.

"I can't drink all of these and eat food too."

"These drinks aren't food, they are medicines designed to keep you alive. Your heart has already been damaged through lack of food", Chris replied.

Once again I was stunned and, for one brief moment, began to realise how ill I actually was.

Hospital hours are long. It was well after 11.00 pm before I was given my final medication. I was on anti-depressants and vitamin and mineral supplements. Even though I was extremely tired after my first traumatic day, I still couldn't sleep. For a second night I listened to the town clock strike each quarter of an hour, hearing the cries of the patients in the padded cells.

Early the next morning, a male nurse entered my room. It felt strange because I was incredibly shy and hadn't spoken properly to men of my own age ever before. James was the first male nurse I'd met. He brought me my mid-morning Build-Up drink, saying he would sit with me as I drank it.

I was still having great difficulty drinking these thick milkshakes and started my usual round of apologies for being so slow. James, who was about 24, just smiled a lazy smile, saying I should take as long as I needed. He couldn't think of a more pleasurable job, sitting on a chair, talking to a pretty young girl while she enjoyed a drink. Pretty girl? I was shocked. I thought back to the electrician at my work in the solicitors' office. He had told me I was gorgeous.

Who were they talking about?

"Not you!" said the voice.

My parents visited me every day for the first three days but on the fourth day, Mum and Dad were stopped in the corridor and taken to the nurses station. The doctors in charge of my case had decided my parents' daily visits were not necessarily beneficial and could even slow down my recovery. Mum and Dad were stunned. Was the hospital saying they were in some way to blame for my anorexia? My parents, as usual, complained to me but never said a word to the hospital authorities.

Ironically, the next morning a letter arrived for me at the hospital, from Gran.

"Dear Anna,

Your Mother phoned me today and said that now you are in hospital at last, they finally have their lives back. You always were a total burden to them and they only allowed you to stay with them to keep up appearances. They really want you to die. They don't love you. You are nothing but a weight around their necks. Don't let anyone see this letter. Tear it up as soon as you have read it because if you show it to your Mum and Dad, they will just agree with me. They will tell you they don't love you.

Gran."

I read and re-read the letter many times before tearing it up just as I'd been told.

The staff at Trengweath hospital had been given my Mum and Dad's version of my 'Grandmother'. My parents said Gran was to blame for much of our family's problems. But as the doctors had not actually met Gran, they couldn't be certain she wasn't just an imaginary person my parents had invented, to cover up their own uncaring behaviour. My Grandmother's absence left the hospital in considerable doubt..

How much were Mum and Dad responsible? Perhaps only God will ever know.

Looking back today, I have so many conflicting emotions. So many different answers to the same questions. I love my parents but then I think 99% of all children do. Our parents are the first contact we have after leaving the womb, as we arrive on this planet.

It was my decision not to eat, but who originated the voice in my head?

Why did I get the voice and not Mark my brother?

Who continually sent the eight year old Anna to Gran's?

Who was so blind, not seeing what was happening at my Grandmother's?

Could anyone be so blind?

Should Dad have shouted at me about the blocked drains or just put his arms round me?

For better or worse, my parents were instructed only to visit once a week.

The following days merged, as I became familiar with the hospital routine. Weekdays passed more quickly, with doctor's rounds, etc. Weekends, however, stretched out. They were more varied. With the doctors off duty and longer visiting hours, this meant lots of strange faces about.

As time passed within the security of the hospital, the voice quietened slightly and I developed a rapport with many of the staff, especially the male nurses. Miraculously I was actually talking again, something I hadn't done properly for so many years, and some of the nurses became good friends.

Whenever one male nurse, called Stuart, was on duty, he would come up to my room to say hello, even if he had been assigned to another ward. He liked me and appeared genuinely thrilled by my progress. On the very first day, he saw me walking to the washroom. He called out:
"Whoah, my little Anna's up and around at last, there'll be no stopping you now. I'll have to warn all the boys in town."

Stuart always congratulated me every time I gained a pound in weight, and although I would diminish my achievement, saying it was the food I'd been given, he quickly counter replied:

"No it is all your hard work. We provided the food, but you were the one who fought the panic attacks and the paralysing feelings of fear and managed to force it all down. Anna, you deserve tremendous praise for your bravery."

I liked Stuart but found his compliments very hard to accept because I hated gaining weight.

I had to learn however to accept that weight gain was good for me, not bad. Somehow, I needed to realise getting heavier was opening the gateway to a new life for me. As long as I remained underweight, my life was restricted, and at that stage I couldn't even walk to the toilet unaided.

Even though I knew weight gain was essential, I still had the same old phobia, afraid that everybody was noticing how huge I was now becoming. I felt so ashamed. I was growing bigger every day. My anorexic brain could not understand that the difference between 6 stones (84 lbs.) and 6 stones 1 lb. (85 lbs.) was imperceivable. For me, gaining just one pound made me feel like I'd grown enormously overnight, and the whole hospital was talking about how fat I'd become.

I was now seeing Dr Ken Carlston every two or three days. He had set me a target weight of 7 stones (98 lbs.) before I was allowed off full bed rest and it was safe to start walking about. I asked if I would be discharged home when I reached this set target of 7 stones (98 lbs.)? He looked uncertain, saying that going home was a long way off yet.

His uncertain reply shattered me, and after he left, I sobbed uncontrollably. I literally cried non-stop for several hours and the nurses, unable to console me, called Dr Ken back to the ward.

This huge man came back and sat, trying to comfort me. To console me, he came up with a new offer that when I reached 7 stones (98 lbs.), we would draw up an official contract.

The contract would allow me home permanently if I signed an agreement to achieve certain weekly target weights set by the hospital. Failure to reach the agreed targets, while living at home, meant an immediate return to hospital. I was now 6 stones 6 lbs. (90 lbs.) in weight, so there was still a long way to go and, gaining one pound a week, this meant eight more weeks stay in hospital.

Around this time my roommate, Cath, left the hospital. In her place, came an older woman suffering with agoraphobia. Immediately she commented on how thin I was. Our new daily conversation became:
"Look at your arms - they're like matchsticks."

A short time later, my official bed rest was over and I was permitted to get up and walk about the hospital. This presented new problems. I was shy and found it hard to talk to the other patients. A few days later, the doctors decided on another major deal that said from now on, I had to eat in the canteen. For me, this was very intimidating. I didn't want to eat food at all, let alone have to ask for it myself. The catering staff all knew I was anorexic and automatically checked off my food

every meal time. In front of long queues of other patients, I had to show a card stating my dietary requirements. There were endless discussions with the canteen ladies.
"You must have two potatoes and cabbage."
"Oh no", I would reply
With these arguments going on, all the patients in the queue behind me got more and more uptight and every meal time, I felt so humiliated.

The weeks passed and to a degree I became more self-sufficient, which meant my regular nurses were able to turn their attention to other duties.

More problems soon arose however. When first admitted, I was adding weight quite quickly but now, several weeks later, any increase had slowed down considerably. Initially I'd put on 5 lbs. in the first week, mostly because my body was re-hydrating itself. During the weeks following however, I only managed a further two pounds and Dr Ken wasn't happy with my speed of progress. I was also personally very dissatisfied. I knew, at this rate, I would be in hospital for a lot longer. Always looking to encourage and spur me on, Dr Ken decided I needed a goal to aim towards and came up with the idea that a weekend's leave would be an appropriate incentive.

I thought the scheme wonderful, and really excited, couldn't wait to tell my parents on their next visit. Their reaction, however, totally devastated me.

Mum didn't want me home at all. She didn't think I was strong enough to leave the hospital, even for a weekend. I still barely weighed 6 stones 7 lbs. (91 lbs.)
"I can't look after you", she went on.

My Mother's rejection, the unwanted feelings, this was the story of my life. All the old pain resurfaced. My Father may well have wanted me home but, as usual, did exactly what his wife wanted.

In spite of my parent's attitude, Dr Ken still went ahead and arranged a meeting with Mum and Dad that Thursday morning, to finalise the proposed weekend leave. I had to promise to eat everything on my diet plan, taking plenty of rest while at home. My weight was to be monitored before I left and upon return to hospital. I don't know exactly what Dr Ken said to my parents, but after about half an hour's discussion, Mum and Dad came out agreeing I could go home for my weekend's trial.

I was over the moon, totally ecstatic to be going home and seeing Windrush again. I had spent nearly four weeks locked up in that hospital, looking out of my bedroom window for hours on end at the suicide railway viaduct.

The decision over my weekend's leave was made late that Thursday afternoon, leaving only one day to wait before my parents actually collected me. Excitedly, I watched the clock all day on Friday and couldn't wait for Mum and Dad to arrive and collect me.

The drive home was wonderful. The whole countryside looked beautiful and I felt so free. As we turned into the drive of Windrush, I began crying. I had never thought I would see my home again. Our car pulled up and my two cats obviously heard us arriving. Both tripped over themselves as they raced in to greet me.

I spent the morning sitting on the patio deck chair with a book, looking up occasionally to stare out at the deep blue sea. Being at home felt amazing. For the first time in years, I enjoyed a semblance of contentment. Even the thought of lunch time approaching failed to fill me with the usual fear and anxiety.

Maybe I was getting better?

Maybe…

The nurses at the hospital had given my parents six sachets of Build-Up, with strict instructions I was to have three each day, in addition to my normal meals. On Saturday, Mum enquired what I wanted for lunch, and together we worked out the exact amount of food I would eat. Anything was better than the hospital. I hated it there. I realised to stay at home I needed to get heavier, and for the first time I actually wanted to put on weight and believed I could do so. My parents were amazed at the amount of food that I was able to eat. They hadn't witnessed my gradual progress in hospital, so to them it appeared I'd gone from eating virtually nothing to half size portions overnight. I could see the happiness on their faces when they saw me eat almost normally.

After lunch on Sunday, obeying Dr Ken's instructions, Mum and Dad suggested I went to have a lie down. I fell asleep quite calmly but woke up in a fit of depression and panic. Realising in two hours I was going back to the hospital, I began to cry and both Mum and Dad tried to comfort me, saying how well I'd done and that soon, if I kept up the good work, I could come home permanently.

Before I knew it, Sunday evening arrived, and it was time to return. My parents tried to cheer me up but the drive back to the hospital was very distressing emotionally. I was so despondent.

"Why do I have to go back?" I kept saying.

I'd proved I could manage to eat by myself now. I didn't need the hospital any more.

Back at the hospital it was all very emotional and my parents dropped me off at my room, leaving almost immediately. Two nurses appeared, taking me to be weighed. I was full of trepidation. This was the moment of truth. If I'd lost weight, I would not be allowed home again. Staring at the scales, it seemed an endless wait as the needle settled for the nurses to read exactly what I weighed.

The result was wonderful. I'd put on half a pound in the two days I'd been away. We all celebrated as if we'd won the lottery. Both nurses were overjoyed, and so was I. This was actually the first occasion in my entire life I'd been happy to put on weight. I was winning the battle against anorexia.

Was I beating the voice, or was it just biding its time?

Feeling strong, I decided on Monday to ask the doctor if I could now return home permanently.

"See? I can do it. It's better for me at home", I kept repeating to myself out loud.

Early the next morning, Dr Margaret arrived in my room. She was very pleased with my progress but couldn't commit herself as to whether I'd be allowed home or not.

The decision could only be made by Dr Parkinson, the head consultant.

Dr Ken had just been filling in while Dr Parkinson was on holiday in Australia. It was Dr Parkinson who was ultimately in charge of everything.

I would be seen by this "Big White Chief" the following day. He, and only he, would decide if I could leave.

Everything was spinning around in my mind. I didn't know if a change of doctor was to be a good or bad thing. At least I knew Dr Ken. He was kind and understanding but he was also very cautious concerning my condition. He didn't want me to leave until I was at least seven stones (98 lbs.).

All day I rehearsed what I was going to tell them. I was going to say how important it was for me to look after myself. I would emphasise how I felt I'd let my parents down for so long and how I now wanted them to be proud of me. My speech was endless. Even I began to believe it.

Early that Tuesday morning I was officially summoned to Dr Parkinson's clinic. It was quite strange really. He seemed young for a consultant psychiatrist, probably in his early forties. He looked smiley and seemed to joke with the patients each time he called them in. I waited my turn, with my stomach somersaulting. For comfort, like a baby holds its teddy bear, I clutched my glass of Build-Up in my hand.

At 11.00 am Dr Parkinson came out to collect me and took me into his room. I felt very uneasy, seeing all my notes spread out on a table in front of him. Smiling, he asked me:

"What's that drink you're holding? Is this a meal fortifying drink?"

"Yes", I replied.

"Hmm", he said. "I'm not sure that I like you being on those. Really what I want you to eat is normal food. These supplements don't train your body to accept the correct amount of food it needs," he said, shaking his head. "We'll start cutting down on them as soon as possible."

I liked this doctor already. Anyone who would stop me having the dreaded Build-Up drinks had to be alright. Dr Parkinson then asked me how I viewed my anorexia and staying in hospital. I told him about my weekend's leave, saying I'd managed to eat normally for the whole two days and actually put on half a pound. I explained how unhappy I was in the unit and told him, if I was allowed to go home permanently, I would eat better because I would be happy at home. Hearing myself speak, I sounded very convincing.

He looked down at my notes.

"It says here Dr Ken Carlston suggested 7 stones (98 lbs.) as your target leaving weight. What are you now?"

"6 stones 7½ lbs. (91½ lbs.) " I replied.

"Hmm, well you're not quite there yet are you?"

"No", I agreed "but I'm certain I could continue to make better progress at home. In fact, without the stress of being in a hospital, I probably would put on weight more quickly."

He stopped to think about all I'd said and looked back over my notes.

"You've been depressed since you arrived. They've increased the dosage of anti-depressants quite considerably haven't they? Tell me, how do you feel now? Are you still depressed?" he asked.

"Oh no, I'm not depressed any more, I just want to go home", I pleaded.

"Look, I'll tell you what I'll do. I'll talk with Dr Margaret, your keyworker, later this morning. If she feels your health might benefit from spending some time at home, then we'll have a meeting with your parents this afternoon. Don't get your hopes up but I'm beginning to think that perhaps this hospital environment is no longer beneficial to you."

I couldn't believe what I was hearing. Dr Parkinson, was on my side. I liked him immediately. Leaving, I picked up my Build-Up drink and was just about to say goodbye.

"Oh leave that drink here", he said. "You really must drink these within half an hour at the most, otherwise bacteria starts to breed. We don't want you going down with food poisoning do we? I'll have a word with the nursing staff. If they make you any more of these, they must be with ice-cold milk and are to be drunk within thirty minutes."

I practically danced out of his office. I felt so good. There was a chance he'd let me home. I was so excited and couldn't wait to tell my parents. Rushing to my room to find some money for the payphone, I bumped into my nurse Chris on the stairs.

"Oi you!" she said. "Walk. You know you mustn't run anywhere yet. What are you so excited about anyway? This is the happiest I've seen you in ages."

I told her all the news.

"Oh wonderful Anna", she said. "We'll all keep our fingers crossed for you. If Dr Parkinson asks us any questions about how you're progressing, all the nurses are on your side. We'll vote for you. We'll tell him just how brave you are and what an amazing job you're doing. We'll all wear badges with 'Let Anna Go Home'", she joked.

I grabbed my purse and walked slowly down the corridor until the nurse was out of sight, then I virtually leapt down the stairs. When Dad heard the news, he was thrilled at the thought he might have me home again soon. Mum however, was far more cautious. She seemed uneasy about taking over the responsibility of caring for me.

The meeting was set for 3.30. Dr Margaret came up to my room to tell me Dr Black, two nurses, my parents, along with Dr Parkinson and herself would attend. I was anxious. Could I cope with so many people in one room, all firing questions at me and discussing my case? For me, it represented a grand jury and my trial for treason.

My parents arrived, and together, we waited outside the conference room for the toughest ordeal of my life.

At 3.30 sharp we were all called in.

I walked into a room awash with doctors and nurses, all sitting around an enormous table. All eyes were on me. My fight to go home was about to begin.

Dr Parkinson began the meeting, explaining that each person in the room was to give their individual opinion. I was first to speak and was asked to explain why I thought it beneficial for me to leave the hospital.

"I put on ½ a pound last weekend and if I was allowed home, I would eat more and put on weight quicker." I confidently announced.

My speech went on for ages. Dr Margaret spoke next and I was quite surprised by her comments. She was very pleased with my progress but felt I would benefit from a few more weeks in hospital. I was dismayed. No wonder she hadn't talked to me in my room for long that morning. She knew how depressed I was. She knew the good progress I'd made at home. Why was she suggesting I stay in the hospital?

One by one, each person spoke, and as they did their views echoed around this room.

When Dad's turn came, he said how proud he was of me, and had absolutely no problem having me at home again. He'd watched me closely over the weekend and observed how well I dealt with food. We all listened to the views of the nurses, who congratulated me on my progress, saying how much all the staff loved having me but would miss me.

Mum spoke last. She did not seem to be as positive. In so many words, I could feel her trying to persuade the panel to keep me in hospital. I was petrified this would undermine Dr Parkinson's ultimate decision. Here I was, so close to leaving hospital, and now my Mother's opinion could ruin everything. On and on she went, repeating her fears that my weight was still dangerously low. It was abundantly clear to the entire room that my Mum did not want me home.

At this stage, the voting was equal. Dad, Chris and Rachel were for me going home. Dr Black, Dr Margaret and Mum were against.

The entire case rested on the Big White Chief.

The moment of truth had come.

Dr Parkinson's views differed quite considerably to Dr Carlston's. The Big White Chief believed my body had adapted to being at such a low weight. I was now very unlikely to suffer complications if I started to do gentle exercise such as walking. He didn't feel I was 'at risk' any longer.

When he finished speaking, Dr Parkinson said he would like to have a discussion with his staff privately to make their decision. They left the room.

The jury was out.

Dad smiled at me, quietly saying he was proud of the way I'd presented my case. Dad's kindness was very moving that day but I was, once again, deeply hurt by Mum. She had betrayed me. She privately praised my behaviour over the previous weekend and then, faced with the doctors, she did a complete about turn saying she didn't want me home. The voice in my head was shouting:

"Your Mother hates you! She really doesn't want you back in her house!"

Fifteen minutes later, the jury came back.

"And your verdict on Anna is…?" I said in my mind.

Dr Parkinson had reached his decision. He spoke softly, telling me that I would be allowed home on a week's trial, but there were some very strict conditions. I had to see Dr Margaret at her out patients clinic in Helston twice a week and would be weighed on both occasions. If I made progress and put on weight each week, I would be allowed to remain at home. If my weight dropped, however, I would have to return immediately, the very same day, to Trengweath Hospital. It was a very simple contract.

Amazingly, Dr Margaret announced there were no weighing scales whatsoever at the Mental Health Clinic in Helston, so it was agreed I should use the weighing machine in Boots, the local pharmacy. Those public weighing scales gave a read out ticket, so I could prove my weight to Dr Margaret each visit. Everyone agreed this was a satisfactory arrangement and I was told I could go home immediately.

I was dumbfounded. After all the time I'd spent in hospital, my discharge had come so suddenly. I had no time to think and couldn't really take it all in. Half an hour later, another nurse arrived to find me packing.

"I just heard you're leaving", she said. "We are all so pleased you're going home, but we'll miss you."

I packed my bags in a few seconds flat. I couldn't get out of the hospital quick enough, in case the doctors changed their minds. Within minutes, I was down the stairs and into the nurses station. They all hugged me and wished me well, telling me I could phone any time I needed.

Driving away from the hospital, sensing freedom, I kept promising myself all this would never happen in the future. In the car, as we drove home, I kept repeating over and over, I would never allow anorexia to overwhelm me again. Whatever happened, I would fight it constantly and never be re-admitted to hospital.

How wrong I was.

I didn't realise my fight with Anorexia nervosa was far from over.

In fact, it had really just begun.

Chapter 15

ON PAROLE

It was May 1991. I was nearly 24 years old. Waking up the morning after I'd left Trengweath hospital was exciting. I was free. My freedom, however, was contingent on the amount of progress I made but I felt secure. I honestly believed now I would never again cut back on the amount of food I ate. In my mind it was simple. I had to eat to stay out of hospital.

I was convinced my stay in hospital and 8 pounds extra in weight meant I was now cured of anorexia. I knew that I had to attend the out patients clinic twice each week and see Dr Margaret but this didn't worry me. Somehow that morning it felt as if, by some magic, I'd been given permission to eat again. I would now eat like a normal adult woman and everything was going to be okay.

It was all so simple. I was better.

But was I?

I hadn't counted on the power of the anorexic voice.

"You are out of hospital now. You're overweight and very fat."

As agreed with the Hospital, before each appointment with Dr Margaret, I was to weigh myself in the local pharmacy. For me, this represented power. In the past, whenever I was weighed, the doctor would see the result before I would, whereas with this set up, I would be first to know. I liked this. I was in control.

I remember my first out patients appointment on a Wednesday in early June 1991. It didn't matter what I weighed, because I had a foolproof excuse even before I stood on the pharmacy scales. Dr Parkinson had already pointed out the pharmacy scales would be different to those at the hospital. No two sets of scales ever gave identical readings. He had said it wouldn't matter what the reading was on this occasion, any drop in weight was down to the variation in scales.

Looking down at the read out, I was shocked. I weighed almost exactly the same as I had the week before, but this time I was wearing more clothes and shoes too.

What was happening?

In my very first week at home, I had lost weight!

At exactly 10.00 am, grasping my weight printout, I entered the Helston Mental Health Centre for the first time. I didn't really understand why I had to see Dr Margaret so regularly but I felt safe knowing that after each appointment I was free. It wasn't like being in hospital, I could just get up and walk out of her room.

The inside of the centre was like a rabbit warren, with corridors leading in all directions. I was shown into a nearly empty room, with just two low lounge chairs and a small coffee table. The walls were plain, apart from a loud ticking clock.

At our first meeting, Dr Margaret just asked me how I felt about being discharged and how I was coping with things at home. She arranged to see me twice a week on Tuesday and Friday mornings, telling me about the work we'd be doing together. It was all quite relaxed. Towards the end of the meeting, she casually asked me for my weight slip. Dr Margaret glanced at it and then, looking at me, first said nothing. Eventually she spoke.

"Well Anna, we'll have to keep a strict check won't we?" I didn't reply, not knowing if this was meant to be a threat. Nothing more was said. Arranging to see me three days later, she wished me goodbye and saw me out. I was very relieved that morning to say goodbye but felt extremely unsure about future visits.

I walked from the health centre to the local coffee bar, where I'd arranged to meet my parents. Strangely enough I was quite excited. I'd been into coffee shops before but had remembered them with feelings of extreme discomfort. It was quite weird but that day, coffee shops didn't seem such a terrifying prospect and I actually relaxed, sharing a piece of ginger cake with my Dad. Eating the cake was fine but as soon as I finished, my mood changed. I felt guilty. I could hear the voice again.

The terror had restarted and somehow my difficult thoughts around food slowly but surely, started to re-surface.

"What are you doing eating cake? Do you want to get even fatter?" the voice screamed.

For the next few days, more out of fear, I followed my hospital diet plan quite strictly. However, soon I began to rebel. Dr Parkinson had wanted me to put on one pound each week but the voice became more domineering, and ordered me to aim for only ½ a pound.

"Half a pound is more than enough", said the voice

It was June 1991 and, within a week, the voice got louder and my calorie intake was already slipping. My options at meal times at home became more limited. Mum wasn't bothering to cook huge puddings like I'd been having in hospital, so each day I settled for fruit, which was far fewer calories.

Gradually, the voice began plotting and planning new ways of making me lose weight.

"Butter is out of the question."

None of the deep-rooted issues that led to my anorexia had been resolved. Until these had been settled, the anorexic voice could reign on unchallenged. What these issues were, baffled me, but with Dr Margaret, I was beginning to find out. I wouldn't speak about my Grandmother's abuse but began to discuss Mum and Dad with the doctor. Our sessions became a competition between the voice and Dr Margaret.

I saw Dr Margaret twice a week on a regular basis now. We spoke mostly about my home life. She always questioned me about my relationship with my parents. I clearly remember one of her questions:

"Can you tell me of an incident when you felt very hurt by your Mother's behaviour? When you felt you really didn't deserve the treatment you received?"

I just can't understand if it was guilt, fear or shame but I could not accept my Mother had done any bad things to me. Only after repeated requests, bordering on cross-examination, did I eventually manage to tell Dr Margaret something about just one isolated incident.

It happened one Sunday while my brother Mark was visiting. I went into the kitchen to get ice cubes. My hands were shaking and I dropped everything on the floor. Mum shouted:
"You are so clumsy! Look at that mess you stupid thing!"
I started crying.
"Do you ever do anything right?" my Mother sarcastically asked.
I felt terrible, and after gathering the ice cubes, I ran to my room and locked myself in. Crying hysterically, I started hitting myself on the chest. I remained upstairs in a terrible state for an hour, before my Mother even came up to see if I was alright.

The ice cubes had been just one instance. There were so many more that I couldn't or wouldn't talk about.

As the weeks passed, my memories of hospital started to fade. I did nothing all day except sit there, staring into space, or occasionally read or embroider. I began to feel safer at home and the voice began to issue fresh commands.

"That hospital made you very fat."

Once again, it dictated the foods I could eat. I started counting calories. Nothing had changed. It was all going downhill once more.

"You've got to eat less."

At first I changed my breakfast cereal to a lower calorie brand and then I stopped spreading butter in my sandwiches at lunch, the filling became low fat. The dieting was quite subtle to start with, I didn't want anyone to notice. The changes may have been small, but quickly, they had a dramatic effect on my weight.

On the Tuesday of my third week at home, I discovered my weight had stabilised. It reached 6 stones 12 lbs. (96 lbs.) but there it stopped. I felt very nervous that morning as I went for my usual appointment with Dr Margaret, petrified I would be re-admitted to Trengweath because there was no weight gain. Here I was, after only three weeks at home and now, I could be forced back to hospital.

The possibility of actually going back to hospital hit me extremely hard. For a second time, I sincerely promised myself I wouldn't ever diet again.
"What am I doing?" I screamed to myself. "I've just been released from hospital. Oh God! What's happening?"
I had to do something quickly to convince Dr Margaret I had tried to put on the weight.

Amazingly, on that visit, Dr Margaret was in fact very understanding. She wasn't surprised my weight had stabilised, saying this would often happen in the early days. It just meant I had to increase the amount I was eating. She suggested I add a yoghurt to my diet each day. Promising her I would do so, I left the Health Centre very relieved I was still free.

"I've had a reprieve", I sighed to myself. "Now, I must tell my parents, so we can buy some yoghurts."

I walked to the usual coffee shop where I regularly met my parents after each doctor's visit, quite prepared to tell them what Dr Margaret wanted. Halfway down the hill, it all changed. The voice started quite quietly, whispering insidiously in my ear.

"You're not really going to tell them about the extra yoghurt are you? Don't tell your parents about the change. They rarely talk to Dr Margaret. The doctor thinks they're responsible for your problems anyhow."

The nearer I got to the coffee shop, the louder the voice shouted. As I opened the door and walked towards my Mum and Dad, the voice blocked out everything else. I tried to speak about the yoghurt but the voice sent an electric shock wave through my head, stunning me into silence.

"Be quiet, say nothing."

All I could say was:
"Dr Margaret thinks I'm doing really well."

As soon as the voice heard those words, it started to release its grip, praising me for my behaviour.

"You did well. That was good."

For the rest of the morning I was very quiet and Mum, sensing something was wrong, asked me if the doctor had said anything else.

"Yes", I replied. "Dr Margaret was worried that my weight has stabilised."

Mum was annoyed.

"Stabilised? Oh no!" she said, panicking.

Frightened of my Mother's reaction, I wished I hadn't spoken.

For the next week I didn't eat any extra food, certainly not Dr Margaret's extra yoghurts. Even though I had promised myself I wouldn't diet any more, I couldn't stop cutting calories. When I weighed myself at home the night before my next appointment with Dr Margaret, I was mortified to discover not only hadn't my weight increased, I'd actually lost a pound. The voice, however, was thrilled.

"Well done, but you've still got a lot more weight to lose."

The voice knew I had to do something quickly before I weighed myself in the pharmacy. If the ticket showed my weight had fallen, I would be instantly re-admitted into Trengweath where they would fatten me up. I fretted all night, until the next morning the voice came up with a very simple solution.

"Wear heavier clothes."

I was supposed to wear the same clothes each time I was weighed but before this weighing session, I altered my clothing to make sure the new ones were heavier. The biggest change of all, though, was to my shoes. I swapped my light canvas ones for some new heavy chunky sandals I'd just bought. It was the first time I'd worn them. I hoped everyone would just think I wanted to wear my new shoes. They weighed at least half a pound alone.

Half an hour later, I stood on the scales in the pharmacy, shaking like a leaf, hoping my weight had not fallen too dramatically. The printout finally appeared, declaring my weight identical to the previous week. I now knew for certain my weight was falling and prayed to God this would not be obvious to Dr Margaret.

On that visit, Dr Margaret first commented about my shoes and clothing. Whilst pleased I'd spent some money on myself, she noticed how heavy and chunky my shoes were.

For some reason, during our meeting, this week Dr Margaret was vague and distracted the entire time, forgetting to ask for my weight slip until the very end. When she saw the reading was the same as the week before, she asked whether I'd been eating a yoghurt each day. I couldn't lie and made excuses, going round and round the subject, but said I would try harder in the coming week. Dr Margaret, seemed satisfied with this answer, and made no more comments about either my weight or clothing.

Somehow, over the next few weeks, everything continued with my weight neither going up nor down.

It was about three or four months later that Dr Margaret made a very mysterious announcement. Late in July 1991, she told me another person would be sitting in on our next session the following Tuesday. I wasn't to feel worried. I just had to say at the end of our meeting whether I liked the new person or not. What was happening? What was going on? Was it because I was doing so badly? I panicked. Why would Dr Margaret want to involve another doctor?

I was anxiety ridden for the four days prior to our next appointment. Who was this new person Dr Margaret was going to introduce me to? Why did I need to see someone else? What was going to happen? By now I trusted Dr Margaret and had just begun to talk openly with her. I didn't want it all to change.

Early in August 1991, at our next appointment, Dr Margaret saw me alone first, telling me she would introduce me to Andrea Brandon, a Community Psychiatric Nurse. The idea was for us all to talk together for a while, to enable me to assess whether or not I was going to feel safe with Andrea. I was required to say if I thought the new nurse could help me.

Dr Margaret then told me, she herself was about to leave the Clinic. She'd only been there on a placement as a trainee doctor and was now moving to another hospital!

Trainee doctor? I couldn't believe what I was hearing!

I was stunned. I hadn't realised Margaret was just a trainee doctor. Why wasn't I talking with a proper doctor? What was going on? I was being looked after by a student.

Now I was being passed to a psychiatric nurse.

What next?

Were they going to give me to the hospital porter?

Discovering Margaret was a student upset me and took away all my hope. I now felt totally alone.

The voice came back as an expert, not a trainee.

"So Anna, you've been fooled again, talking to a student!"

"You are so stupid! Stop eating and all will be well."

"Stop eating stop eating!" the voice screamed.

I listened.

Chapter 16

QUIETLY DYING

Once Margaret left, I started to see Andrea regularly
every Monday morning. For my first appointment,
Andrea visited me at home. After introducing herself to
my parents, she then spoke with me alone in the lounge.
Andrea was very thorough. Once again, I had to go
through the whole sad story and repeat all the information
I'd already told Margaret about my childhood, college
days and secretarial work.

Andrea wanted to see me alone and found it extremely
irritating when my Mother constantly hovered around,
frequently bringing in cups of coffee. Mum wouldn't give
up trying to involve herself in our conversation.
Eventually, exasperated, Andrea asked her to leave and
closed the door behind her. As with Dr Margaret, I totally
glossed over anything about the abuse I'd received from
my Grandmother, which, even at the age of 24, I was still
too scared to talk about. After a month's assessment,
Andrea decided that Cognitive Therapy would perhaps
help me to beat the anorexia.

Cognitive Therapy involves recognising you're thinking
in a negative way and changing your thought processes.
All of our feelings are a response to a thought. If the
thought is negative, the resulting feeling will be negative
- sadness or depression. Andrea explained to me that if I
could change negative thoughts into positive ones, the
resulting feeling should be good rather than bad.

Once familiar with the theory behind Cognitive Therapy, Andrea gave me numerous printed sheets headed 'Thoughts and Moods Diary' to fill in each time my mood changed and I felt bad.

At first, the mood swing diaries were regularly updated, but soon the voice screamed:

"Put that stupid book down!"

From then on, the entries were limited. This intense therapy continued for several months, with varying degrees of success. Sometimes we made good progress but then the voice cancelled out all the good. It was often three steps forward and four steps back.

Time passed, but making little headway, Andrea herself grew more and more despondent and decided to try something new. She enlisted Alan, an occupational therapist. That January, I met Alan for the first time. He was 35, a very cheerful and robust Welshman, who seemed permanently happy. It was his job to try to help me integrate myself back into the outside world.

On our first meeting, Alan told me to choose a task I really wanted to do but hadn't done for ages. He and I would then do it together. Ironically, I decided I wanted to make a cake. I loved cooking but hadn't practised for many years, always afraid I would be expected to eat some of the food.

The following Wednesday morning, Alan came to our house bright and early to help me bake our cake. He made himself at home, putting on music and making coffee. The encounter I had wished to avoid, unexpectedly became a pleasurable experience.

"Well Anna, look at our beautiful cake", Alan smiled. "Are you going to eat a bit?"

"Just a little", I said nervously, tasting the freshly baked cake.

After this I started seeing Alan every Wednesday. He regularly took me out. We did many activities together, from sitting on the top of a cliff painting the scenery, to playing with his kittens at his house near Lands End. Alan became more of a friend than a therapist. He believed his main task was to take me out of the house as much as possible. Alan could clearly see that, over the years, I had became too wrapped up with, and dependent on, my Mother and Father. He wanted to show me there was life outside my parent's home. I was an anorexic hermit. Alan wanted to make me like a normal 25-year-old girl, going out to discos and nightclubs.

By my next appointment with Dr Parkinson, my weight had fallen quite dramatically. The doctor was worried and annoyed at the same time. He was now running out of options and, as a last resort to prevent hospitalisation, he decided to try family therapy. It was his desperate last attempt before applying to the courts to have me sectioned and forced into hospital.

Dr Parkinson instructed Alan and Andrea to be the therapists in charge. I was scared of family therapy and tried so hard to convince Dr Parkinson to give me another chance to tackle the anorexia alone. Dr Parkinson, however, was adamant. He was certain now that family therapy was the only way forward. It was either that or hospital.

The first of the family meetings, which were all held at home, was a total disaster. I spent the entire session trying to make myself as small as possible in my chair, while everyone discussed me as though I wasn't there at all. My parents, Andrea and Alan argued amongst themselves about what was best for me. My Mother, as usual, had so many bright ideas that all centred around me going back into hospital, while the others favoured me staying at home. It was so humiliating. I hated it. I often felt, with everyone talking for me, they were discussing the habits of a sick pet dog.

My parents found these sessions heavy going and very threatening. Both Mum and Dad felt Alan and Andrea were pointing the finger, accusing them of causing my anorexia. Both my Mother and Father became sharply defensive but one remark from Alan, aimed at my Father, sent him into a fit. Alan accused him of being over-protective and Dad stormed out of the room, as my Mother shouted:
"Are we on trial now?"
That turned out to be the last family session we had.

Following that incident, Andrea now had less and less respect for my parents' involvement and now insisted they took a step back and didn't pressure me to eat anything. Up until then, my parents had often taken the lead and tried to force me to eat the meals they set in front of me. I felt tremendous relief when Andrea said from now on, she alone was in charge of what I ate. I welcomed the decision. With my parents out of the picture, it felt like some of the monsters had gone.

It was during this year, I felt what was probably for me the worst ever family rejection. My brother Mark had met a woman called Gail, and after a whirlwind romance, they became engaged. Gail had been married once before and was 13 years Mark's senior. Both Mark and Gail didn't want to have a long engagement and were planning to get married within a few months.

As soon as the wedding date had been set, a fierce debate started. Andrea, my nurse, was unhappy about me travelling back to Southend for the wedding. She argued with my parents, saying I probably wouldn't survive the trip.

"Her weight is so low now she is at serious risk of having a heart attack."

Andrea pleaded, saying I shouldn't be walking any more, let alone going to a wedding 400 miles away.

"Your daughter is far too ill to make such a journey", she insisted, as she was leaving that day.

I was scared of returning to Southend anyway, because my Grandmother would be at the wedding. I was very upset and couldn't believe that my parents would want to spend a whole day with that woman. What was I supposed to do? Have a photograph taken smiling with my Grandmother? Was I expected to eat at the reception as well as meet many new people? I did not want to go, but as usual, my guilt took over. It was my own brother getting married and I had to be there for him.

It was obvious I was ill and at the time, my parents were undecided if I should go or not go. Although concerned for my health, the most important factor was that we all appeared together as a family. After much discussion, it was decided we would all go, and Mum started to plan our outfits. This in itself was very difficult for me. I couldn't bear to look at myself in a mirror any more. I felt so fat, in spite of the fact by this time, I weighed barely five stones (70 lbs.) but all I could see were rolls of fat.

When Andrea found out I was travelling 400 miles, she was furious, but my parents wouldn't budge. My nurse tried right up until the day we were leaving to get me to change my mind, but under emotional pressure from Mum and Dad, I just had to go.

On the day we were due to leave, I packed my case and watched Dad load it in the boot with theirs. I had woken that morning feeling shaky but had put it down to nerves. With the cases in the car and us ready to go, I suddenly felt this strange pain in my chest. I sank down onto one of the hall chairs. Dad found me and wanted to carry me out to the car but I refused, telling him I was too ill to go to the wedding.

"I can't go, I just can't", I pleaded.

I wasn't going to be able to stand for a long time in a stuffy church and then meet lots of strangers.

There were numerous protests as Mum and Dad tried to persuade me to come with them.

"Come on. You can rest in the car. We have to all be there for the photos", Mum went on.

Eventually realising they were getting nowhere, Mum and Dad just left me alone and drove off to Southend. Alone in that bungalow with just the sound of the sea, I felt totally deserted.

A different pain filled my chest. An intense, agonising longing to be loved. I understood they didn't feel able to miss Mark's wedding - it was too important, more important than I was. Since I was a baby, I never felt sufficient love from Mum and Dad. This void was filled with my anorexia, like others escape into drug and alcohol addiction.

I believed I was finally dying. As I waved good-bye to my parents, I wondered if I would ever see them again.

Four days was a long time to be in the house on my own. Andrea and Alan were under the impression I was going to be in Southend with my parents. Neither, Mum or Dad had bothered to phone Andrea or Alan to say I hadn't gone with them, so they were both unaware I was home alone.

With no other distractions, the anorexic voice was now free to reign in my head.

In the kitchen I found one of our cats sitting by her bowl, waiting for food. If only eating was as simple for me. "I'm hungry, therefore I eat", said the cat. The voice spoke next, giving its orders telling me not to eat anything for the next four days.

"Now is your chance to really lose weight."

I went back into the lounge and sat in my chair, which seemed to be getting larger. The chair wasn't growing. I was shrinking. On the television was a daytime chat show about loneliness. I started to cry. I was so unwanted. I knew that my brother Mark was more important to my parents than I ever could be. He always had been. I tried to make excuses for my Mother and Father. They'd promised Mark they'd be in the bridal car and take Gail to the church. They couldn't miss their only son's wedding. But I stopped to think. If my daughter was dying would I leave her alone for four days?

The true answer to the question was so painful.

That cut was the deepest.

Without breaks for any meal, the day stretched on indefinitely. Eventually it began to darken and I started to feel scared. The black dreams of my childhood with Gran still haunted me. I crept around the house looking in all the dark corners, petrified someone had sneaked in during the day when the doors were open. I was convinced someone was hiding in the shadows, waiting to pounce.

That night, staying awake for as long as possible, I watched television but finally my eyes couldn't stay open any longer and I drifted into a nightmare sleep. The same recurring dreams I'd had all my life came back. Visions of murderers breaking into the house and hacking off my limbs tormented me, until I awoke drenched in sweat, screaming for help. As the dawn broke, I made myself a cup of black coffee. This was all I would allow myself. The cats, hopeful of an early meal, rubbed around me as the kettle boiled.

Taking my drink, I returned to bed and began to write on a big white card. I made a chart showing every hour that was left until 7.00 pm Sunday, when my parents were due back. If I ticked off each hour as it passed, maybe the time would pass more quickly and I'd get by.

The second day was just a haze. My stomach now rumbled painfully but the discomfort felt good. I hadn't eaten for 24 hours and I was starting to feel very spaced out. I made myself another cup of black coffee but as I walked back to my chair, my legs gave out and I slipped to the floor, spilling scalding black coffee all over me.

My parents phoned me only once throughout the entire weekend. Late that Saturday evening they called and practically the whole conversation was about the wedding. They excitedly told me about the video they'd taken, discussing Gail's wedding dress and the reception. I listened, with tears rolling down my cheeks.
"Shouldn't they be asking about how I feel?" I thought.
I'd always wanted them to love me. Why were my Mum and Dad not home with me when I was so ill?

The last two days merged together, as my time chart became more crumpled, but religiously I still ticked off each hour as it passed.

Nearly 72 hours without food was now taking its toll, somewhat deranged and high on no food, I left the house to walk on the cliffs. Alone with the sea breeze blowing in my face, I walked towards the edge. The voice started screaming.

"You'll never get married! You'll never get married! You're too fat! You're too fat!"

I must have stayed out on those cliffs for several hours, and it was nearly 6.00 pm when I slowly made my way back to the bungalow. In the garden, I fell over and had to crawl back through the open French window, dragging myself onto the couch.

A short while later, my parents returned. I heard them opening the front door and calling out to me. Now I had to appear cheerful and happy. I didn't want them to know how bad the last four days had been. If they discovered how desperately ill I had become, they would definitely arrange for me to be hospitalised immediately. Somehow, I had to look good.

I smiled at Mum and Dad, forcing myself to appear well but they weren't completely fooled - my face was without colour and my eyes were smudged black. After numerous questions, my Father got me to admit I had felt ill and had not eaten as much as I should have done over the last four days. Mum made me a cup of soup and brought me a roll. In front of them both, I forced myself to sip at the drink, whilst nibbling at the bread. The food somehow revived me slightly. I wanted to go to bed but my parents encouraged me to stay up so I could watch the video they'd taken of Mark's wedding. It all made me feel so despondent, knowing I would never get married. No man would ever want me - a useless, screwed up mess of a person.

I didn't really watch the video properly and just sat there in a dream. As the film finished, my parents both went to

bed. It was still quite early but Mum had a migraine and
Dad was exhausted from the 400-mile trip. They left me
alone again with my thoughts. Images of wedding
dresses, cakes and bridesmaids filled my head. This
would never happen for me. I got into bed and buried my
face into my pillow, praying I wouldn't wake up in the
morning.

The next day, on Monday morning, I just wasn't strong
enough to go out to visit Andrea at the Health Centre so
instead, she came to visit me at home. She was furious,
finding I'd been alone, and immediately phoned Dr
Parkinson. Together they decided to call in the
Community Treatment Team (CTT). This was a twenty
four-hour, seven-day a week, emergency crisis care team
giving intensive home treatment. They were called in to
help if a patient was seriously ill but refused to be
admitted to a hospital.

Andrea told me a nurse would visit every day. They
would come and see me at lunchtime, actually sitting
with me while I ate. I now realised my life was in danger.

I was numb. I didn't want to see a nurse each day but Dr
Parkinson was adamant. It was either the CTT or
hospital. I had little choice and reluctantly agreed that the
treatment team could begin visiting immediately.

For the first few weeks, I saw various different members
of the CTT and then, shortly before Christmas, I was
visited by Clive - a specialist member of that team. I
liked Clive immediately. He was an extremely kind,
gentle, understanding, supportive and trustworthy man.

At 34 years old, he was attractive, with a smile that was both reassuring and cheeky.

Clive explained he wanted the treatment to work on a negotiation basis, with me taking more responsibility for my own recovery. I was very weak by now and only spoke in whispers. In response, Clive found himself lowering his own voice until together, in hushed tones, we negotiated a plan of action to follow for the next few days.

My first task from Clive was to identify the foods I was prepared to try to increase.
"I'll eat more plain yoghurt", I would say
"Okay, it's on list", Clive would reply.
Then he suggested how much extra I should eat. Negotiations were very intense but in whispers. We haggled like big city dealers, throwing figures at each other for hours until we finally agreed.
"An extra banana with your meal?"
"No."
"Extra pear?"
"No."
"Extra half yoghurt?"
"Yes"
Deal done.
We would shake hands. Another meal had been agreed.

Throughout this time, I talked sparingly to my parents about my latest treatment. Mum found this frustrating and stopped Clive as he was leaving one day. She told him she was very unhappy that he talked with me but not with her about my treatment. Mum also offered to provide her own 'background information' on myself and the family.

Clive, however, explained patient/client confidentiality meant he couldn't discuss my case with Mum and suggested she asked me personally about our sessions. I trusted Clive but there was no way whatsoever I could discuss with him or anyone exactly what my Grandmother had done to me.

It wasn't Mum who told me about her chat with Clive - I heard it from him. Now I really began to worry. Mum was still sending out mixed messages. She was telling me she was happy I was at home but at the same time, saying to Clive I should be in hospital. Now I really didn't feel safe. Certain Mum wanted me out of the house, I started to spend all my time listening as Mum cornered Clive each time he arrived or left. A side effect of anorexia is acute hearing. Although my parents were whispering about me, I could hear what they were saying, even from another room.

I worked with Clive for several months. This was unusual because the CTT as a rule were only called in to work with a patient for a very short intensive period. Clive, however, was adamant he didn't want to drop my case and endured many fights with his bosses in order to continue working with me. I found out much later, it was Clive who kept me out of hospital.

He visited me every day, arriving at the house before 8.00 in the morning. We not only concentrated on food but we talked about my personal goals and, through role-play, explored my past relationships with my Grandmother and my parents. Clive demonstrated ways of expressing and asserting myself within my home but whenever I tried to assert myself , I always failed. I couldn't state my own needs, fearing the overwhelming disapproval from my parents. I was the ultimate people pleaser.

While I steadily lost weight, becoming smaller, the voice grew in size, it's power developing as my health deteriorated.

"You'll get fatter if you listen to Clive."

By March 1994, according to the scales in the pharmacy, my weight had stabilised at 5 stones 11 lbs. (81 lbs.) In reality, it was falling at quite a steady rate but I was keeping it level by carrying more weights in my pockets each week.

I amassed small change until I possessed a huge collection, wrapping the coins in tissues to prevent them from clinking together. I then taped them into plastic bags, hiding them in my pockets every time I was weighed.

As my weight dropped, I simply increased the amount in my pockets. Eventually I reached a stage when my jeans were so heavy, I could hardly keep them up and had to tie lengths of string around my waist to prevent them from falling down.

I was constantly petrified that Dad, Mum or Andrea would notice my jeans were hanging strangely so each time I returned from a weighing session, my first job would be to rush to my room to change and quickly hide the coins. After each weighing day, I carefully put my coin stock in the back of a drawer ready for the following week. As time passed, I became more and more afraid of being caught. Now I was carrying nearly 12 lbs. in weight in my jeans.

"You'll never get caught, we've got them fooled."

Nothing changed and my weight continued to fall until in April 1994, Clive could see the state I was now in and finally gave up. His treatment wasn't working.

It was do-or-die time and Clive, now desperate, somehow as a last resort, persuaded me to hand over control of my diet to him. Instantly his role changed. Now he became the master, telling me what I had to eat as he stood over me. I could no longer decide anything for myself. In front of me each day, Clive now measured out the exact amount I was required to eat. I tried to eat everything Clive set out but sometimes I took up to two hours at each meal sitting and I never finished the food.

My health was now deteriorating more rapidly than ever before. My weight on the pharmacy scales read 5 stones 8 lbs. (78 lbs.) but, in reality, I weighed 4 stones 12 lbs. (68 lbs.)

My life was in danger.

My Grandmother. My Parents. The Voice.

They had all contributed in pulling me down to life's basement.

The lift stopped here.

Andrea, daily watching my weight diminish, was by now seriously concerned that I could actually die. She telephoned a specialist in eating disorders - Dr Jill Welbourne. They both treated the matter as a life or death emergency and put me on a liquid diet of high calorie food supplements for the next five days. By now, I had reached a stage where my body could no longer utilise solid foods.

Early the next morning, Andrea phoned, telling me that it was out of her hands - a group of doctors had officially taken over my case. My weight was now so low it was certain that, without intervention, I was going to die.

I was stunned, hearing the words:
"We need to admit you immediately into a specialist hospital."

It was happening all over again. Hospital!

Andrea informed me an appointment had been made for me to see Dr Parkinson the next day. I put the phone down, sobbing. My parents looked at me baffled, desperate to know why Andrea had phoned. I couldn't tell them, crying so much I was unable to speak and stayed in bed the rest of the day.

The following morning in Dr Parkinson's surgery, I sat there dumbfounded as he explained he had secured a bed for me in a private clinic in Bristol. I was to go as an NHS patient, so the private fees were waived.

The doctor went on to explain that Heath House was a new, quiet and small hospital set in wooded grounds. I would be looked after there until my weight had reached a safe level. The hospital ran a program of intensive therapy for anorexic patients, ensuring a high success rate. He insisted it was vital I went into hospital the very next day and had arranged admittance for two days later.

The tremors started as soon as I heard Dr Parkinson's decision. I had battled for nearly three years to avoid hospital and now I was to be re-admitted. I was numb.

Clive arrived early the following morning. We talked alone for a while and I could see he was very sad. He had been hired to help me avoid hospital but had failed. He was visibly upset. So was I.
"Where did we go wrong?" Clive said.
Clive asked me to write to him from the hospital to keep him updated and, giving me a hug and a kiss, left me to pack.

After a few brief words with my parents, Clive left. Seeing him drive away, I realised my last hope had vanished. I was leaving Cornwall for a Bristol hospital, this time perhaps never to return.

The end had come. I was losing weight faster than I could control. Even if I ate now, the weight still dropped off.

The voice wasn't talking any more.

It was laughing. It had done its job

"Well done Anna!"

WASTING AWAY

CLIVE

Chapter 17

BRISTOL HOSPITAL

Heath House was located in Bristol, 200 miles from our home. We set off early that Sunday morning, stopping twice for breaks. On both occasions my parents collected the drinks, bringing them out to the car because I wasn't strong enough to walk into the restaurants. Hot chocolate at the first stop and soup at the second. The soup actually tasted wonderful. It was the first savoury food I'd had in five days.

"Don't start enjoying all that food", the voice came in.

We arrived at Heath House at about 2 pm. Set in forested grounds, the drive to the hospital main doors was a steep and winding hill. From the outside, Heath House looked similar to a very grand country hotel. I opened the car door, gently placing my feet on the gravel but my legs folded beneath me. I collapsed in a heap on the drive, grazing my knee as I fell. With nothing to cushion my bones, the fall was excruciatingly painful. Looking up, I could see two nurses running towards us. They lifted me, carrying me in the front door, where they gently placed me in a wheelchair.

I was ill. Dangerously ill.

The thick carpet deadened the sound of the wheels as I was silently ushered into the ward. It was surreal, unlike any previous hospital. The reception area was a grand hall with a sweeping staircase. If there hadn't been nurses around me, I would have believed we were in a luxury mansion.

I was wheeled past the nurses station, taken to a private room and laid on the bed. The room, complete with television, lounge chair and en-suite bathroom was so unlike a hospital. Lying on the bed, my eyes were now closing. I was so tired and at this point, I thought I was going to die. Could I surrender now? I'd fought for so long. I was extremely low. Why couldn't I just go to sleep forever? I could hear people speaking in the corridor.

"We have to get some fluid and nourishment into her very quickly. This one is close to the edge, we don't have much time. Set up an intravenous drip into her arm immediately."

I wondered who they were talking about. Maybe another anorexic girl in the hospital?

"Anna's her name", I heard someone say.
They were talking about me.

A doctor in a white coat walked into my room, introducing himself as Dr Holland. He smiled. I tried to do the same but just stared back blankly. He was quite handsome, about 30 years old with blue sparkly eyes and a reassuring manner. Sitting on the bed beside me, carefully reaching for my wrist, he took my pulse. There was a look of deep concern on his face.

"I need to do an examination and we have to weigh you", the doctor said. "Relax. Don't worry I will be careful. You are very fragile and we will bring in a special set of scales so you can sit on them. I'm sorry to make you do this but it is essential we know your present weight."

Slowly, the doctor continued with the examination, taking my blood pressure, temperature and then testing my reflexes but with no response. Eventually he gave up. My body was slowly shutting down. I started to feel faint. The room was beginning to sway.

A short while later, the scales were wheeled in. The doctor carefully lifted me from the bed, sitting me gently in the seat. My parents had told the doctors I weighed 5 stones 8 lbs. (78 lbs.) I watched the needle on the scale move. Eventually it came to rest at 4 stones 10 lbs. (66 lbs.) It was obvious now I'd been lying to everyone for a long time about my true weight. The doctor, however, wasn't angry. He just lifted me back to the bed, assuring me I was safe in his hands.

My eyes were closing. I was passing out.

A nurse was standing in the corner of my room and the doctor walked over to talk with her. I heard his words.

"Her pulse is very faint and her blood pressure extremely low. So is her temperature. She's excessively dehydrated, we need to get fluids into her fast. Go and collect the I.V."

The doctor returned to my bedside to insert the drip but I was losing consciousness. Images of my Gran filled my head. I was a child again. I could see the plates of bony fish and fatty meat she'd forced on me at meal times. I could hear her taunts.

"Eat the food, you horrible fat child. Fat and ugly, that's what you are. Fat! FAT! FAT! FAT!"

The words spun around my head, becoming louder each time. I reached up to cover my ears with my hands but couldn't move. An I.V. had been attached to my right arm and I hadn't even felt the needle entering my bony flesh.

Opening my eyes, I saw my Mother and Father were about to return home. They were leaving behind a tiny shadow of the daughter they'd once known, now weighing less than a young child.

I could hear the doctors talking in the corridor, trying to reassure my parents.
"Yes, she's in a bad way but we'll get her better. She's safe now."

As soon as my parents had gone, the doctor returned to explain that the consultant, Dr Branson, who was due to examine me, had a throat infection. She couldn't risk coming too close, fearing she might pass on any germs. My examination would now be delayed until the next day. At that stage, even a minor infection could have killed me. An hour later the other nurse, Clare, entered my room, to sit with me for the evening. I drifted in and out of consciousness, hearing her voice chatting away every time I opened my eyes.

The past and present merged. It wasn't Clare who was beside me but my Grandmother. She was smiling but her eyes were cold. I shivered involuntarily and cried out. A hand touched me. I jumped. A voice spoke to me.

"Anna, Anna, Come back to us. You're in hospital. It's me, Clare."

Time passed and it became night. The nurses changed shift and I was introduced to the night staff. They took my blood pressure and temperature, then made me a milky drink, sitting with me encouraging me to take tiny sips. Throughout that first night, I was in and out of consciousness, not really aware of my surroundings.

For two days my life was hanging in the balance, nurses checking my blood pressure and temperature constantly. Periodically I was woken to be given Build-Up drinks, my drip being re-filled regularly. With each hour that passed, a little more strength returned to my body. Now my inner senses somehow wanted me to carry on. Deep down I still had the will to live. Was this the turning point for me?

Had I actually faced death and won?

On the fourth or fifth morning, I woke feeling somewhat brighter. The I.V. had been removed from my arm. The night staff were just leaving. With the morning shift of new nurses came Lorna. She was 28, somewhat pretty with a mass of curly hair. She told me that she would be my keyworker. It was breakfast time and she was carrying a bowl of muesli.

"How about something to eat?" she said, smiling. "The doctors have removed the drip and if you can manage some food, you won't have to have a new drip re-inserted."

She sat beside me as I tried to eat. The bowl of cereal overflowed and, even though I was starving, the usual feelings of panic engulfed me. I hadn't eaten solid food for six days now and the sight of this meal was overwhelming. It took me forever to finish the cereal but while I struggled to eat, I learnt a great deal about Heath House from Lorna.

The hospital had only been open for about six weeks, which was why everything was brand new. It was a small building with only two wards - one upstairs, one down, housing a mere 44 patients. The dining room, art room and a variety of therapy rooms were situated away from the wards, in the main house. Heath House was the most up-to-date anorexic unit in England.

Nearly an hour later, I finished my first meal and felt like my stomach was about to explode. No sooner had I taken the last mouthful, when Lorna came back with a huge glass of Build-Up drink. It's just like eating in a restaurant, then asking for the bill but instead of the bill, you get served with the same meal all over again. Do this ten times and you'll come close to understanding how I felt.

Food, food, food. All I did was eat.

It seemed like an endless supply of sandwiches and Build-Up drinks followed each other. Lorna returned with lunch - more sandwiches, this time cheese and tomato. I now found out that the doctors had written me up for five Build-Ups per day.

Another Build-Up followed lunch, the third came in the middle of the afternoon. At five o'clock came another sandwich - egg. While I was actually eating, Lorna held a stethoscope to my stomach to check my intestines were working properly. This was a peculiar, unnerving experience and it certainly didn't make eating any easier. She was, however, pleased with my progress and praised me.

"Do you know how close you came to dying Anna? If you'd stayed at home one more day, I don't think you would have survived."

Late that afternoon, I saw the physiotherapist. My body by now was in bad shape. The physio explained that she was going to visit me each day, in order to ensure my muscles didn't waste away while I was on bed rest. Very frail, I imagined, as she exercised my joints, my arms and legs would just snap off in her hands.

That day was busy, and as the physiotherapist walked out, the Occupational Therapist walked in. Her name was the same as mine, Anna. I liked her from the start. She was 29, very cheerful, appealingly scatty and had wonderful blonde hair. We talked for quite a while, as she asked me many questions about my illness and how my feelings were concerning food.

Anna explained that for a while I was too weak to join the main therapy groups. Instead, she would visit me daily with different art supplies to keep me occupied.

"We'll get you painting. Are you any good?" she asked, smiling.

After agreeing I would try, she left, calling back:

"See you tomorrow."

My first week at Heath House was very busy, with each morning dominated by numerous medical tests. With my weight so low, Dr Branson had insisted I have a complete medical examination each day. Re-feeding an anorexic patient can be difficult and, of course, dangerous. Blood had to be taken almost every day too.

Heath House was a private psychiatric hospital that didn't possess all the necessary medical equipment the big general hospitals had. It was because of this, I was frequently taken by ambulance to the other Bristol hospitals for various tests. One afternoon, Lorna accompanied me for X-rays and a C.A.T. (Computer Aided Topography) scan, a horrible experience. A C.A.T. scan is a procedure able to X-ray the brain. I was scared but Lorna wasn't allowed into the X-ray room, so during the scan, I was left alone with my demons.

I was made to lie flat on a moving conveyor belt, with my head kept still in the same position, using foam cushions. The test took over an hour. Throughout the test, I had to remain absolutely still. The examination was divided into two halves. First my brain was photographed as it was, then I was injected with a coloured dye. This dye coloured certain parts of my brain, enabling clearer detailed information. The brains of anorexics often shrink and the doctors needed to see how much shrinkage had already occurred in my case.

At the end of the first week, I met Dr Branson for the first time. She was in her early forties, extremely well groomed and thin. I looked at her, thinking:
"If I reach my target weight I'll end up fatter than you." This seemed unfair. Why was a doctor allowed to be thin and not me?

During our first meeting she was very friendly and tried to ease my mind, explaining all decisions regarding food increases would be made by negotiation only.
"We won't force food down you", she said, holding my hand.
Dr Branson encouraged healthy eating and had decided my diet was to consist of fresh fruit, vegetables and other healthy foods. However she also asked me to name my favourite food. When I said crisps, she added one packet to my daily diet. The idea of adding crisps was to help me to understand I could eat anything I wanted, when I wanted. To show me, as an anorexic, no food was ever off limits. They were treating me like a child of two years old, which I suppose I was when it came to eating.

This child was being asked to eat different foods for the first time.

I'd been in the hospital for about a week when I met Zoë. The nurses had specifically encouraged her to visit my room and introduce herself. I looked up one evening to see a thin and pretty young girl, nervously standing at my door.
"I just wanted to introduce myself", she said. "My name's Zoë and I'm anorexic too."

We chatted for about ten minutes. She told me she was now a day patient, though she had previously been an in-patient for six weeks. She was currently at Bristol University, doing a four-year degree course in Quantity Surveying but still came to the hospital for several hours each day. That evening, she was going to cook a meal with one of the nurses. This was the first time I had met another anorexic. It seemed odd. She appeared so normal. I found it all too difficult to comprehend.

During my stay in hospital I often had long conversations with Zoë, when we talked about our illnesses and the voices in our heads. It was now I discovered that all anorexics had voices in their heads and Zoë and I discussed our voices as if they were close relatives. She and I told each other when our voices were talking to us when we were eating.

"Is your voice talking to you now?" Zoë would ask me. "Mine is. It is telling me that I just must not eat this food."

"Yes, mine is forbidding me from eating this meal too", I replied. "What shall we do?"

The sad part was that we didn't know what to do. None of us realised the voices were imaginary. To all anorexics, they are very real voices that you actually hear, just like the radio or someone talking.

For two more weeks, I was kept on complete bed rest before being allowed to go to the lounge. By now I had become very used to my room and didn't want to leave the safety and solitude I had there. Cheryl, a young nurse's aide, my second keyworker, helped me on that first day to walk to the lounge. I was wobbly but Cheryl was still able to introduce me to the other patients, about five in all. That day, there was only one other anorexic patient in the lounge. Her name was Mary. She had just spent many months at Marchwood Hospital, gaining two stones in weight but was now unhappy with her size, desperately wanting to diet again. Although physically, weight wise, she now looked healthy, psychologically she was very sick. We didn't speak much but just stared at each other. I spent about an hour in the lounge, playing Pictionary with the other patients but, feeling uneasy, was glad when the afternoon was over and I could return to the solitude of my room.

Gradually, during the next few weeks, I walked around the hospital on my own and got to know every corner of it. A week or so later, the doctors decided it was time for me to join the other anorexic patients in the dining room at lunch times.

In the dining room, anorexic patients were expected to sit on a separate table, with a nurse helping them to deal with their feelings about food. For me, this was not a helpful part of the treatment at Heath House. Anorexics can be very competitive and this proved to be a serious problem. We all had our own diet plans and were at different stages in recovery. Meal times were dominated with us all making comparisons about what we were eating. Whenever two patients were following the same or similar plans, arguments would start if one believed she had more on her plate than the other. Eating became like a battlefield. Food was often sent back to the kitchen, with us all convinced we'd been served more than expected. The kitchen staff had specific instructions as to portion sizes but frequently made errors, and chaos ensued.

"You've got fewer peas than me."

"But look at my cabbage."

The meal time disputes went on and on.

I hated the hospital but one day at Heath House was far worse than all the others. After 2½ months, I weighed 6 stones 4 lbs. (88 lbs.) but still I felt huge, like the fattest person ever. Early one morning, Dr Branson told me I was going to have my official medical photographs taken. The idea behind the photos was that I would be so shocked by the pictures, I would never want to return to such a severely emaciated state again. By this time, however, my anorexic brain made me feel larger than ever, even though I was only 6 stones 4 lbs. (88 lbs.) I couldn't bear the idea of being photographed looking so fat.

During my first few weeks in hospital, I had been too ill to go to the medical photographer at the Bristol Royal Infirmary, so my original photo session was postponed. I was furious that morning because, by now, I believed I'd put on so much weight that the hospital wasn't going to bother about the photos. What was the point in taking the pictures? I didn't need photos to see how fat I'd become. All my arguments were in vain and, under protest, I was taken by ambulance to the main hospital in Bristol.

Having those photos taken was, for me, the most humiliating experience of my life. I was only allowed to wear a pair of knickers and was told to climb into a white exhibit style box. Beside me was a measuring stick and I was ordered to stand facing forwards, backwards, then to my right and left sides. The photographer stood half way down a cavernous empty room, hidden under her camera. I felt like a criminal, having a semi-naked mug shot taken. The whole procedure was terribly sordid.

Dr Branson tried to put my mind at ease and promised me that she and I would be the only people ever to see the photos, but it didn't help. I hated it all.

Two days later, Doctor Branson showed me the photos. Seeing pictures of myself was a major shock. There was no denying the photographs were of a girl grossly underweight. Because they were photos, it was impossible for me to doubt the proof in front of me. I could look at my body and see rolls of fat but for some reason, the camera couldn't lie. In the photographs I saw a dangerously thin girl, looking desperately ill.
"Was that girl me?" I kept asking myself.

I found looking at the pictures confusing because it was confronting me with an issue that the voice denied. The voice told me the girl in my picture was fat.

"Look at that fat girl", the voice taunted.

It was a strange confrontation with the voice because there was photographic evidence in front of me, saying the opposite. The picture was of an extremely thin girl but that girl couldn't be me. Just like the voice told me that my body was fat, the voice now tried to convince me the girl in the picture was fat.

The photos were a major issue with all the anorexic patients. One afternoon, Susan, another anorexic, came into my room crying. She said she'd just been shown her medical photos and now felt immensely fat. I tried to explain to her that she wasn't large at all. In fact, Susan was so thin, her veins had collapsed. She was being fed through a naso-gastric tube since she would no longer agree to eat voluntarily. Already she'd pulled out this tube twice. Once, emptying her drip down the sink, the nurses caught her. She was sectioned at Heath House for a year.

Susan wanted to show me the photos. I could then give her my honest opinion on them. What I saw totally shocked me. Susan was dying. She was as emaciated as a concentration camp victim but she couldn't see this. Patiently, I tried to convince her she was dangerously thin. I even found magazine photos of models, trying to point out and compare how much larger they were to Susan. She looked at the models, repeating she just wanted to be thin like them. In other anorexics, I could see what was blatantly obvious - a girl dying of anorexia yet convinced that she was fat, it didn't make sense.
"If only I could be as thin as her", I thought to myself.

Susan wasn't the only anorexic girl in the hospital to turn to me for help. As soon as I was well enough to go to the dining room, I began helping the other patients. I would talk constantly to them while they had their meals, trying to convince them that they were allowed to eat. Before long, the girls would fight to sit next to me.

"Anna, the voice in my head is telling me that I am a bad person and that I am not allowed to eat this potato. What shall I do?" Ann would say.

I then explained to her that the voice was wrong. She was allowed to eat, she was a good person and deserved food.

"The voice is just trying to destroy you, Ann. Don't listen to it. You have your whole life ahead of you, you are only 17. Don't spend years, like I have, listening and obeying a voice that talks rubbish."

I would challenge Ann and Katie to eat foods they had never before eaten and though terrified, they realised it was only the voice that was stopping them from eating, and would accept my challenges. Sometimes they failed but mostly they won through. Amazingly after six weeks, Ann had begun to feel comfortable around food again. Her periods had re-started and she was well on the road to recovery. She was one of the lucky ones. Her anorexia was diagnosed early before the voice had taken total control. It felt wonderful that I was able to help both her and Katie so much.

Even though I knew the voice was lying to Ann and Katie, I was still unable to understand that it was lying to me. It was still my master and ruler.

Initially I had been discouraged to start therapy until I weighed seven stones (98 lbs.) because the doctors believed my level of concentration wouldn't be high enough. However, as soon as I reached six stones (84 lbs.), Dr Branson changed her mind. Miraculously my C.A.T. scan had shown no shrinkage to my brain and the doctors, being pleased with my progress, now wanted me to join some of the therapy groups. It was Anna, the Occupational Therapist, who sat down and discussed with me which groups would be the most suitable.

As time passed, Anna commented on how mechanical I was. I never expressed my feelings. I knew the theories of all the groups and the therapy but was like a well-versed recovery machine, on emotional auto-pilot. Never was I able to voice the pain I suffered with my Grandmother or the deep disappointment resulting from my parent's lifelong lack of concern. It was early one Wednesday morning when my breakthrough came. On Anna's instigation, I was attending the drama group. This particular day, I was the only person in the group and Anna had something unusual planned.

She set up a tape recorder to play some special music. Anna went on to tell me that all the doctors and nurses didn't think I was in touch with my real feelings. Due to some childhood trauma in my past, I'd learnt to block out my pain by becoming anorexic. Her job was to get me to accept the pain I felt and let it out. Until I did, I would never recover. Anna told me to just sit and listen to the music she was going to play.

REM's 'Everybody Hurts' started playing. I was overwhelmed. The words were so powerful, with one of the lines being "When you're sure you've had enough of this life, well hang on." Before the song was even half way through, I had tears running down my face. The effect the song had on me was life changing.

For me, the beginning of my recovery had started that very day.

Could this be my awakening? Could this be my turning point? Could I possibly be getting better? It all looked good but this was life in hospital, a closed safe environment. I couldn't live in here permanently. The outside world was going to be another mountain to conquer.

A day or so later, I received a phone call from Dr Parkinson, telling me he was coming up to Bristol to visit me. He and Andrea were coming together to see how I was progressing. We spoke for a while on the phone and then arranged that they would visit the following Wednesday.

I was actually having a bath on the afternoon that they came, but had quite a pleasant shock to return to my room and find them both sitting on my bed. It was nice to see them again after so long and Andrea had brought me a beautiful bunch of flowers. The three of us talked for over two hours, with Dr Parkinson asking many questions about my future hopes and plans.

At five o'clock, Lorna appeared, to take both Dr Parkinson and Andrea to the conference room. It was only then that I realised all the doctors and nurses were specially meeting that day to discuss my case. Everybody was there - the Occupational Therapists, the Physiotherapists and all the other in-house doctors and nurses. They were deciding if and when I should be discharged.

Later the verdict was delivered. It had been decided that when I reached 7 stones 2 lbs. (100 lbs.) I would be allowed to go home for a fortnight, then return to the hospital for another two weeks. After this I could go home again, alternating one week at home, one week in hospital until my weight stabilised.

I wasn't happy at all. 7 stones 2 lbs. (100 lbs.) was still four pounds away and it could take me a month to reach that target weight.

The meeting ended. The verdict had been delivered and Dr Parkinson and Andrea left. For the following week I was very depressed, as I tried desperately hard to eat as much as I could. But very soon my weight had once more stabilised at 7 stones (98 lbs.) and refused to go up, which made me very agitated.

I battled on and a week later, somehow, I managed to practically reach my target weight, when the latest bombshell was dropped. Dr Branson had changed her mind. I was to be allowed only one week at home instead of two.

Apparently the previous day, Dr Branson had met my Mother for the first time and was shocked at how very thin Mum was herself. The doctor was now very worried about the effect my Mother's weight had on me. Dr Branson was concerned that I would perhaps compare myself to my Mother and decide that eating and putting on weight was wrong once again.

I was confused. What had my Mother's weight got to do with it all?

I was in hospital, not my Mother.

It was too late. All out of my hands. Everything had changed. Dr Branson had now decided that, after this week away, I must return to the hospital for a month, as there was a lot more therapy that still needed to be done. Regardless of all my arguments, there was no changing the doctor's mind and ten days later, I was allowed home for one week only.

That week home was confusing for me. I was very pleased to be home but so many hidden emotions were now flooding to the surface. I kept staring at my Mother, who was very thin, thinking so many things. Why did I have to be fat when my Mother, all her life, was allowed to be so thin? When visiting neighbours complimented me on how well I looked, I took them to be saying how fat I looked.

"Well" equals "Fat" in an anorexic's mind.

When I returned to hospital, depression set in. I hated the place. At home during that week, thank goodness, my weight had increased but over the next three weeks in hospital, it stabilised once more. Ironically the doctors, seeing this, reversed their previous decision. Somehow fate had worked in my favour because during the week at home, my weight had actually increased. The hospital now decided on a one-month trial period at home.

Dr Branson wanted me to return to the hospital after this month to work through any fresh problems I had encountered at home and I readily agreed. I was so happy about going home and, once the decision had been made, my discharge was very rapid. I was interviewed by the dietician and she gave me a strict diet plan to follow, along with a month's supply of Build-Up drinks. I was also given a letter to take to my GP, who I had to see immediately I got home. There were strict instructions however, and during my trial month away, the hospital insisted I would also have to see Andrea each week.

I spent my last afternoon collecting comments and other good luck messages on a huge sheet of card from all the people I knew at the hospital. It is a moment I will always treasure. Some of the remarks are very moving and I felt deeply touched that I was so special to all those people I met at Heath House.

I left hospital feeling good but back home, everything changed.

The power of the voice and my fear of returning to hospital, led me to break the agreement I'd made with Dr Branson. When the time came for me to return to Bristol and talk about the problems I'd encountered, I categorically refused to go back. There were many lengthy telephone conversations with the nurses and Dr Branson but I was adamant. I did not want to continue with my treatment at Heath House.

"Just refuse! Just refuse!" said the voice loudly.

There was no way I was going back.

THE CHAIR I SAT IN FOR FIVE YEARS

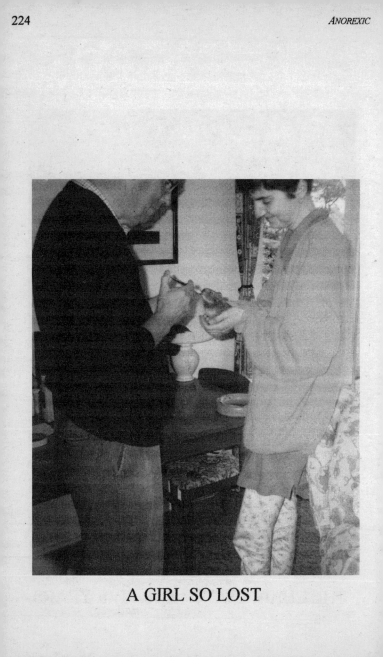

A GIRL SO LOST

Chapter 18

A DYSFUNCTIONAL FAMILY

I was now walking a tightrope because, with my weight dropping, the hospital could get a Magistrate's Court Order to force me, like a criminal, even against my will, to be taken back at any time and kept in hospital.

My mind was split into two parts. One was Anna, who wanted to stay out of hospital, and knew to do so, I had to eat. The other was the self-destructive girl that wanted to starve herself to death. It was that mixed-up individual that was now back home, with two very emotionally sick parents, all living together in the middle of nowhere overlooking the sea. Together with the voice, we all made up a pathetic group of individuals.

The same sick Anna that left Windrush, was now back home.

Anna had gone into hospital weighing 4 stones 10 lbs. (66 lbs.) with a very sick mind, a very sick heart and a very sick soul.

Anna had come out of hospital weighing 7 stones 4 lbs. (102 lbs.) with the same sick mind, the same sick heart and the same sick soul.

Anna's weight was healthier but Anna's emotions were still very sick and out of control. I was 26 years old but inside my adult body was a five-year-old child, imprisoned in front of huge plates of food, still scared of the dark.

You can put an anorexic in hospital, plug them into a drip, fill them with high calorie fortification drinks and yes, they will get heavier. Day by day, drip by drip, the weight chart at the bottom of the bed looks better. So does the patient, sitting up now at the other end of the bed. Their colour returns, the gaunt look disappears and very soon you can take that person out of bed and put them into Occupational Therapy. Feed them and, in between each meal, keep their brains occupied with jigsaws, painting and group therapy sessions.

In that protective hospital environment, sheltered from the outside world, the anorexic learns how to eat normally for the first time in years.

Eating under supervision, however, is just a band aid exercise. A physical recovery becomes apparent but the psychological damage festers on.

I was still desperately ill, sitting on my own emotional time bomb called anorexia. Nobody in my psychological state should have been allowed to leave Heath House. No anorexic patient wants to stay in hospital because staying in hospital means eating and eating means getting fat. The entire staff of any anorexic clinic should never be swayed by arguments from the patient regarding his or her discharge. Because a patient is heavier, that does not mean to say the patient has even begun to get better.

Anybody who's starved down to 4 stones 10 lbs. (66 lbs.) obviously has many deep-rooted problems. It is essential to recognise these problems and to learn to accept, overcome and live with them. In essence, it is vital to find out why the patient became anorexic in the first place. If the anorexic patient's basic issues are not addressed, all you achieve is to return a heavier patient to the same conditions they found unbearable to manage previously. You are expecting them somehow, as if by magic, this time to cope. It's a bit like taking a car with a mechanical fault for a service. Instead of looking under the bonnet, the garage gives it a wash and a polish before handing it back. The car didn't work properly before and, in spite of the external wash and polish, the vehicle still cannot function. I'd had my wash and polish and was back at home, facing real life, not jigsaws.

Nothing had changed and, as before, I was still unable to cope. During the first couple of weeks at home, I lost 5 lbs. in weight and to make matters even worse a letter arrived. It was from Gran.

"Dear Anna,

I don't know why they even bothered letting you out of hospital because you're not going to make it and your parents don't want you anyhow.

Gran."

I'd only been home a short while when Dr Parkinson, who by now had heard about my weight loss from the local clinic, rang, giving me a very strong final ultimatum. He wasn't happy at all and now insisted I was put under immediate close observation. Clive and Andrea, the original two psychiatric nurses who saw me before I was in hospital, were now being instructed to visit me once again each week. Either I agreed to them coming, or he would get the court to force me back into hospital against my will, using the Mental Health Act.

I had no choice. I had to agree and the visits began.

Dr Parkinson instructed both nurses to hold a series of family therapy sessions and, although my parents were very much against it, they had little choice. Mum and Dad had to join in because to refuse, would be showing their lack of interest in the original problems causing my anorexia. Loving parents should always be interested in the problems that cause one of their children to become anorexic, unless they feel guilty and responsible.

The family therapy was a disaster from the start. Fifty percent of every therapy session was my Mother criticising me, saying I was untidy and took up too much space in the house.
"Anna is so messy, she keeps leaving her things everywhere", commented my Mother continually.
Every time the therapist tried to question the justification of her cruel comments, my Father would jump in, making a silly joke to try to change the subject. His wisecracks got so bad, my Dad was actually banned from a few meetings.

At the end of each session, my Mother always asked if it was really necessary for her to attend again. My Mother kept on saying:
"We are not a dysfunctional family. It's Anna who's sick - not us. She's had this illness for so long now. When is it going to go?"

Going to go? Was she talking about the illness or me?

"Don't you think Anna should go back to hospital?" my Mother continued.

"I can never be alone with my husband."

She pulled out a photo of my brother Mark, saying, "Look at our son. He's normal. He's married with a small child. He's not ill, Anna's the only one that's sick."

I was now 27 years old and my entire life revolved around parents who had so many unresolved problems of their own. We were three sick people, living by the sea.

As the sessions went on, the anorexic voice joined us.

"Here we go again", the voice said to me.

Then, in my head, it started to shout at the therapists.

"You're all wasting your time, you know. There is no way we will let you make Anna fat!"

The seasons changed. Time passed by. A lot of time.

The therapy continued and five more lonely anorexic years went by, where all I ever did was stay at home and somehow keep my weight at just above six stones (84 lbs.). In my isolation, even the voice had told me to:

"Keep your weight above six stones, so they don't take you back to the funny farm to fatten you up."

For those long, lonely years, my only activities and contact with the outside world were the regular, same old, two weekly trips out with my parents.

Those five years, one thousand eight hundred and twenty five days in all, were the loneliest and most isolated years of my life. I was imprisoned in solitude on Anorexic Island. The only other inhabitants were a sick Mother and a sick Father.

Our desperately sad lives inside Windrush never varied and followed a strict routine.

My Mother, not needing an alarm clock, woke up at precisely 6.50 every day. Our day began and immediately she woke me and, like an obedient sheep, every day I sat in their room drinking tea while Mum and Dad were still in bed. How many other 28-year old girls sit in their parents' bedroom day after day? On the dot of 8.00, we all sat in the lounge, watching Breakfast TV round the same table, eating the same breakfast. At 8.30, breakfast finished. Then we all officially left the table, with free time until 10.30. During free time, I was allowed to do anything, except go beyond the garden gate. At 10.30, coffee was served back in the lounge. 10.30 until 1.00 - free time within the boundaries of the garden gate. 1.00 - lunch and then free time until 6.00, at which time the evening meal was served. After dinner, we all sat in the same chairs looking in the same direction towards the same television. At 9.30 sharp the television went off, three sick people stood up and went their individual ways. Two heading for the master bedroom where, once inside, they closed the door and me, to my own bedroom, where my door was left wide open. I was still petrified of the dark. I never went to bed later than 9.30 and I stayed there until 6.50 the following morning.

This routine of Anorexic Prison Island never varied, except for the two weekly breaks that came at exactly the same time on exactly the same days.

Every Tuesday morning at 13 minutes to nine, my Father would take the white Mondeo out of the garage. He would then return to the house, pick up the library books from the table in the hall, put them in the boot of the car, close the boot and shout out:
"Are you both ready?"
Dad always repeated the exact same words, it never varied. At ten minutes to nine, we would leave the bungalow. My Mother would sit in the front passenger seat and I would sit behind her. We drove the same ten-mile route into Helston to park in the Library car park at 9.15. Dad and I went into the Library for exactly 20 minutes, while Mum had her hair washed and blow dried in the same style every week. We then walked to the coffee shop, where we all sat at the same table in the corner. We always sat at the same table and on the odd occasion when someone else was sitting at our table, my Father would get extremely upset and be in a very bad mood for the rest of the morning. We always ordered the same three cups of coffee, two cakes and a packet of crisps.

At 10.00, as the Helston Town Hall clock chimed, we stood up and paid our bill - £3.84, exactly the same amount each week. It never varied. From the coffee shop, we all walked to the Bank, where we all stood in the queue and Mum took out the week's housekeeping money, £100.00, never more and never less. We left the Bank and returned to the car park. Depending on the queue in the bank, we would reach the car park at 10.30, then drive along the same road home. We always got back to Windrush at 11.00. The rest of Tuesday in Windrush was the same as any other day, ending at 9.30 pm with all three inhabitants turning left or right to go to their bedrooms.

Thursday was the other big day. At ten to nine, car out of garage, Dad in driving seat, Mum and I took up our official places and we drove in total silence to the supermarket in Penzance. My Father was always much happier if he could park the white Mondeo in his usual parking space. But being a busy car park, those extra happy Dad days were quite rare.

Time of arrival - 9.30 am sharp. With Dad negotiating the trolley like a racing driver and with Mum and I trying to keep up, we zoomed up and down the aisles in numerical fashion one to ten. My Mother carried the shopping list but regardless of whether or not we thought an item would be in that particular aisle, we religiously walked up and down every single aisle. Why we went down some aisles I'll never know because the shopping list never varied. We always bought the same things in the same aisles. Unless of course there was a special offer 'two for the price of one', in which case items were purchased from aisles that we usually drove straight through. I quite liked those weeks, stopping in strange aisles. It livened up the morning and there was always hope of seeing new faces hanging around.

On or before 11.00, my Father pushed the trolley out to the car. He opened the boot, putting the same eight bags of shopping every week into their allotted spaces, closed the boot and returned the trolley to it's rightful position.

Meanwhile, Mum and I took up our respective positions in the car. At 11.05, the white Mondeo left the supermarket and proceeded back to it's home - the garage in Windrush.

This went on without the slightest variation for five years, as the anorexia ripped out my insides.

Within the confines of these strict routines, my parents felt safe. Any change in the pattern of our lives upset the balance and panic would ensue.

Throughout these five years, the loneliness of my anorexic existence grew deeper and deeper. Miraculously, I always somehow managed to keep my weight marginally above 6 stones (84 lbs.) because of the ever-present fear of being hospitalised.

When we weren't sitting having coffee or driving to the supermarket or library, I sat alone, doing embroidery. My Father every day, worked continually in the garden while my Mother obsessively cleaned the bungalow. 90% of my Mother's life was spent cleaning the bungalow. Occasionally Mum or Dad would pass through the room I was in, making some meaningless comment.

Do normal, caring parents allow a 28-year-old, six stone (84 lbs.) girl to carry on existing like that? On reflection I feel that my Father had written me into his life as his eternally young little girl, who in his mind, he could never allow to grow up. As long as I was his little girl, I had to be dependent on my Father, and this continuing fantasy gave him a sense of security. His pet, that little girl so painfully thin, was easier to keep away from other people's attention, in the confines of Windrush. Nobody ever commented on how thin I looked any more because nobody ever saw me now.

Five years is a long time - my parents, doctors, all the king's nurses and all the king's men really didn't look as though they were ever going to be able to put me together again. This ghostly type of existence could have easily gone into six years, into ten years, into twenty years. If I'd lived that long, my parents would have died of old age and I surely would have ended up a lonely, very thin old maiden, alone in Cornwall or more likely dead.

I continued to see Andrea for therapy, weekly. One day she introduced me to Lucy, another anorexic, hoping the contact might help both of us. Lucy was three years younger than me. She had beautiful long blonde hair and I could see how pretty she must have once been. Now, dangerously thin, she just looked seriously ill. Her father was a Naval Commander and, together with her mother, they all lived in a huge house on the naval base with servants that came in to do all the cooking and cleaning. Her parents often held lavish dinner parties and entertained important naval personnel. Throughout her life Lucy had just hidden in her room feeling unwanted. Her Mum and Dad had constantly pushed her into jobs she didn't like. and wouldn't attend any therapy sessions. Anorexia nervosa was Lucy's cry for help but no one was listening. Her parents just thought she was a difficult girl who wouldn't eat.

I liked Lucy and we got on well from the start. We constantly discussed anorexia and I soon learnt that she didn't want to change. Anorexia had become her life.

"Losing weight is the only thing I can do well", she often said. "I love it when people say I am thin. It means I have succeeded. They're wrong when they say I am emaciated though. I am still not quite thin enough."

Horrified at the idea of putting on any weight, she continued to diet. As time passed and her home life became even more difficult she stopped attending therapy altogether and began to drink heavily as well.

One day I went in to see Andrea and she told me she had some bad news.

"It's about Lucy", she said. "She died last night."

I was stunned. I couldn't believe what I was hearing. I'd only spoken to Lucy two days before. At just 27 years old Lucy had a whole life in front of her but now it was all too late. A beautiful and talented girl was dead. Turning to Andrea with tears in my eyes, I started to ask her questions.
"Why Lucy? Why not me? We had the same illness after all. Had everyone tried enough to help her? Had I done enough?"
Andrea tried to reassure me that there was nothing more I could have done.

"Lucy died because she didn't want to fight the anorexia. She wasn't willing to let go of her illness however much we tried to help her."

I understood what Andrea was saying but had everyone helped Lucy enough? It didn't appear that her parents had cared about her at all. I wondered how they were feeling right now. I went home myself, feeling hopeless. Was my life so very different to Lucy's? Was there any point in fighting this illness at all?

To me, that bleak future was already written and it really didn't look as though anything was ever going to change until one night in November 1998.

I experienced a vivid dream.

The following morning, I clearly remembered every word in my dream, I was sitting with a therapist, who was saying to me:

"Food is not the problem Anna.

The problem is you, Anna.

The problem is love. You have never felt loved.

Nobody ever gave you the love you needed.

Love is your problem, not food.

Fall in love and you will want to get better.

Fall in love and you'll want to eat again."

It was like a weird video playing inside my head, where I was saying:

"Yes, but how do I fall in love in the middle of Cornwall? I hardly meet anybody. Who shall I fall in love with? The library attendant? The supermarket cashier?"

In my dream, the therapist paused for a moment, then replied:
"Try joining a pen friend club and I promise you, you will meet someone to fall in love with."

That dream was a magical awakening and suddenly, from a life of emptiness and despair, I had so much hope. When I was fully awake the next morning, I felt so excited, like it was already happening.

I really believed, for me at that moment, a whole new life was beginning.

During the day, I wrote off to a pen club and two days later, I received a list of people to write to. I wrote quite a few meaningless letters to total strangers and over the next week, received several replies. The letters I got back were pleasant enough. Very friendly but they weren't fall-in-love type letters. They were all just pen friend type letters.

The dream came true that Friday in November 1998.

A letter came, which was to change my entire life.

Reading the letter, I instinctively knew that this letter was going to have a dramatic effect on the rest of my life. I read it again and again. This letter read totally differently to all the others.

It was from a very unusual man called Simon.

Reading in between the lines, I felt as if I'd already known Simon for years. I felt Simon was saying he was lonely. He was lost, and even though he never mentioned the word anorexia, he too was in a self-imposed prison. I felt like Simon was desperately trying to say something, just like me, but couldn't express himself. Simon's letter was full of strange stories and odd questions to me. He wrote as if he already knew me. The very last line highlighted Simon's insecurity. It was exactly the same insecurity I'd taken from my Grandmother's bungalow to that very day.

The end of Simon's letter read:

"If you don't feel I'm worth writing to, then you will find this letter fits neatly into most domestic circular bins."

Here was a boy just like me, who lacked self-esteem. This boy made me feel safe. This boy was real, and he made me feel secure enough to write back a real letter. It was to be the first truthful letter I ever wrote. I was going to risk all, telling Simon everything. Inexplicably I knew he would reply to me. I was certain he understood me as I him. I had found my soul mate.

"Dear Simon,

I am usually a very private person and try to never burden others with my problems. I may be wrong but I felt from your letter that you are a sensitive and understanding man. I would like to share with you my deepest feelings. Please forgive me but I have to tell you.

I want to tell you everything about my childhood and how, from the age of three, the abuse I received from my Grandmother caused me to develop Anorexia nervosa. I will understand if you think "Oh no, not a girl with problems, I don't want anything to do with her" and want to stop writing but I feel I need to talk to you."

In a long four-page letter I went on to describe, in great detail, the abuse I'd received and how the anorexia had brought me close to death. I even talked about my stays in psychiatric hospitals, my attempted suicide and the situation with my parents. I held nothing back. Morning came and we went to the library as usual. I posted Simon's letter.

Two days later I was sitting in the same chair, at the same table as I always did, forcing down the same old breakfast. My Mother said:
"You look thoughtful today Anna. Why is that?"
"No special reason", I said, thinking to myself "I wonder if Simon, at this very moment, is actually reading my letter."
It was 8.30 am, and with breakfast over, we all got up as usual and left the table, when suddenly from the hall Dad shouted:
"There's a letter for you Anna."

It was from Simon.

He thanked me for being so honest and trusting him enough to tell him my deepest feelings. In response, he talked of the panic attacks he had suffered himself for years.

"Dear Anna,

A few years back, I hit a depression so deep I didn't think I'd ever feel happy again. It was accompanied by four or five panic attacks each day, which felt like the onset of a heart attack. Each time I thought I was going to die.

Then I read all about panic attacks in a book and realised they could do me no harm. The whole thing was psychological and I decided to confront my fears, a consistent trigger being films relating to death or suffering. I went to the cinema and, sure enough, had my attack, but this time I didn't run away. I let the attack happen. It faded quickly, with each new attack being weaker than the last. Finally they stopped altogether and haven't recurred since. Please write soon ... Simon."

Simon and I began exchanging letters daily. Gradually I told Simon more about my life. He reciprocated, telling me all about himself. His introductory letter had given the impression he lived an active life, juggling many jobs. In reality it was totally the opposite. Just like me, he'd spent most of the last five years depressed or panicking, alone in his bedroom. Simon was hiding from the outside world in London, while I hid in Cornwall.

Excitedly, I was still re-reading his letter 24 hours later when, the next day, Friday morning, another letter from Simon arrived.

It only contained one line and read:

"Please write to me and tell me what you are going to be doing this weekend Anna."

"Oh no", I thought.
The questions about my life that I'd been dreading had started. How could I tell Simon what I did every weekend? How could I say I never went out and that I just did the same things every week with my parents? He wouldn't want to know a freak like me. He'd stop writing.

I'd always found it impossible to lie, so somehow I desperately needed to do something that weekend. What was I going to write and say? That I'd been embroidering all day, or I'd been to the library last week in the back of Dad's car? Or could I write saying we'd bought two packets of washing powder for the price of one in aisle number five?

No, no, no. This weekend was going to be different.

I didn't want to lose Simon.

I had to write, saying I'd done something interesting.

To write about something interesting, I had to do something interesting.

For 24 hours, I planned and planned.

Early that Saturday morning, I opened my wardrobe and, looked at all the brightly colored clothes I'd avoided wearing for years. This was my big day, and excitedly, I chose a yellow jumper. Walking down the hall, I shouted out:

"Bye everyone, I'm going for a walk."

"You're what?" Dad shouted back from the garage. "But it's Saturday morning and we always bake the bread together on Saturday mornings."

"Kay, Kay", he screamed. "Anna's going out."

"She's doing what?" my Mum said. "Going out? But how can she go out on her own?"

"It's true, it's true. She really is going out on her own", said Dad, sounding very bewildered.

"On her own?" Mum replied. "Where's she going? Round the garden?"

"No", I replied. "I'm going out of the garden."

"Don't worry about me, I'll be fine", I said proudly.

The last thing I saw as I left the house was the shock on my parents' faces. I turned at the garden gate and, genuinely smiling for the first time in five years, shouted back loudly:

"See you later!"

I practically danced down the hill to the village. The day was chilly but there was a watery sun in the sky.

"This is normality", I thought to myself. "I have to fight this anorexia. I want to be like other girls my age."

Once in the village, I went into the local shop and bought a magazine and was about to leave, when I noticed the display of crisps.

"Could I buy a packet?" I asked myself.

"NO!" the voice raged.

"Oh yes I can!" I said.

"You're not in charge any more. I am."

"But you'll get f..."

"Just shut up", I snapped back.

"Today I am going to write Simon a letter all about a normal Saturday morning for me in Coverack. This letter is going to come from a normal girl, who walks on the cliffs and who eats crisps like other normal girls."

For the first time in fourteen years, I voluntarily bought a packet of crisps and took them to a bench overlooking the harbour. There, I sat and ate them. It was hard going as the voice tried to bully me continually.

"You'll get fat, crisps will make you fat."

Clutching Simon's letter, I screamed back at the voice.

"Be quiet! Be quiet! I'm eating these crisps, not you. It's my choice what I eat, not yours."

As I forced down each crisp, even louder, the voice shouted, and every time it did, I screamed back.

You could hear my voice above the strong sea breeze.

"I am Anna, Simon's friend. Just a normal girl, and normal girls don't hear voices."

As I walked back up the hill home, I repeated this mantra to myself.

"Normal girls don't hear voices. Normal girls don't hear voices."

As I neared the house, my parents were anxiously waiting at the garden gate.

"Anna! Anna! Where have you been?" Mum asked.

"I just went for a walk."

Without pausing for breath, my Mother went on.

"Is that a new yellow jumper you're wearing?"

"Yes Mum", I said. "It's brand new, just like me really. I'm new today. I've been for a walk. Want a crisp?"

"Where did you get those crisps from?" Dad asked.

"I bought them in the village shop. Do you want one?" I asked again, walking to my room. "I'm just going .to write a letter to a friend", I declared.

"Anna, I've had to make the bread on my own", Dad said, with a funny look on his face.

"Oh, that's great. I'll have a slice when it's baked", I replied, closing my bedroom door.
The sense of freedom that had suddenly come over me was indescribable. I had just tasted life outside of Mum and Dad for the first time ever and it tasted good, damned good.

I knew Simon.

Simon was my friend, not theirs.

I closed my door, to write the following letter to Simon.

"Dear Simon,

I do hope you are having a nice weekend. I am. I put on a new yellow jumper this morning, which I quite like and I've been for a walk to buy a magazine and a packet of crisps. I spent some time sitting on the cliffs overlooking the harbour, watching the seagulls as I ate the crisps. The weather was cold but it felt wonderful to be out in the fresh air. I feel as though my life is turning around. I am starting to leave the anorexia behind."

I finished writing the letter, sealed it, stamped it and coming out of my room, saw it was nearly lunch time. As

I passed my Father in the garden, he looked up totally bemused and said:

"You're not going out again are you?"

Looking back, I could see Mum watching intently through the window. She was in a state of shock. Shaking her head from side to side, I heard her say:

"I just don't know where she keeps going."

"Just slipping out to post this letter", I replied.

"Important is it?" Dad asked, looking puzzled.

"Oh yes", I replied. "Most important. It's to someone very special."

Simon and I wrote to each other continuously. Each and every day a new letter arrived from him. Within a week, parcels began to arrive. Simon, knowing I ate crisps, began sending me dozens of packets with different flavours every day. Invariably the crisps were crushed but slowly I would eat every last crumb. I called them 'my Simon crisps'.

Eating my special Simon crisps, the voice stood no chance. When the voice did speak, saying:

"Fat!"

My reply was always the same.

"No, no, no - these crisps came from Simon and I am eating them whether you like it or not."

During the following weeks, as more parcels and letters arrived, my Dad started to become increasingly annoyed.

At first I couldn't understand why my Father was getting angry. He seemed to be jealous.

"How could my own Dad be jealous of my friend?" I thought to myself.

Soon I began to realise why my Father was jealous. His baby had found a boyfriend. His baby had new interests outside Windrush. His baby was learning to live without her Father.

Dad with his time clock, precision driven life, had always written his dependent anorexic daughter, along with his tranquillised wife, into the rest of his life's script.

He was losing his little girl. Cornwall would never be the same again. My Father was finding it impossible, adjusting to another man being in my life. It made him very nervous.

As Valentine's Day approached, my mind was in turmoil. I didn't believe Simon would actually send me a Valentine's card but I really wanted him to. Neither of us had, up until now, directly said how much we cared about the other one but I wanted so much to send him a card. I bought two special Valentine cards but even after writing different messages on each, I just couldn't summon up the courage to post either card. I kept hearing my Grandmother's voice telling me:

"No man will ever love you."

I was certain Simon couldn't care enough about me to buy and send me a card.

I was so wrong.

The most beautiful card arrived.

Inside, it didn't say 'I Love You' but it was a very affectionate card. I felt cherished for the first time.

The weeks went by, with the letters, cards and parcels of crisps arriving without fail every morning. I'd come alive. I'd been born. I was living. Daily I was opening up and writing to Simon, telling him about my anorexic feelings, and in writing to him, I felt safe. After so many lonely years, I had met someone. A confidante - someone who sincerely cared about me.

My spirits were lifting. I was alive for the first time ever. I was now starting to do what I wanted to do.

Anna was beginning to get a brain of her own.

I no longer went everywhere automatically with my parents. I went for walks on my own, watched what I wanted on television and began wearing different clothes every day. I even went to bed late some nights.

The fight was not over yet though. It was far from over. And one morning, while I was alone at home, a letter came.

A different type of letter altogether.

Chapter 19

THE POISONOUS LETTER

I recognised the writing immediately.

It was from Gran.

"Should I open it?" I thought to myself.

"Yes", the voice yelled. *"You know you want to read it."*

"No, I don't", I replied. "It will only be poisonous."

"Open it", the voice insidiously whined. *"She may be saying she loves you. Isn't that always what you wanted to hear?"*

"Open it!"

"Open it!"

Against my better judgement, I opened the letter, to be hit with my Grandmother's usual torrent of abuse. The timing of her letter had been perfect. With my parents out shopping, I had no one to turn to. Once again, larger than life, that woman - Gran - was with me, telling me how bad I was, telling me how unlovable I was. She'd heard about Simon from my Mum. Now my Grandmother was writing to me to tell me Simon would never love me. She went on to tell me how Simon was just using me and when he got bored, he would stop writing altogether.

I was traumatised and returned to my bedroom for the suicide Stanley knife I always kept hidden in my jewellery box. By now after years of use, the blades were blunt and rusty. But still it worked.

Sobbing my heart out, I slashed both my arms deeper than ever before.

I cut my upper arms very deeply with 10 cm. long slashes, the deepest and longest cuts I'd ever inflicted. Blood poured out from the wounds but I felt at peace as I watched it trickle down my arm. Some seconds passed. Suddenly I began to panic. I'd gone too far this time. I wrapped a bandage around each arm to stem the loss of blood, and then hysterically ran down the road to the local surgery. The doctor, Jenny Parson, was on duty that morning and saw me immediately. It took numerous stitches in both arms to stem the bleeding.

Dr Jenny Parson had always been interested in my case but had never been directly involved because her colleague, Dr Parris, had always seen me. That day, after treating my arms, she really wanted to see what had led me to do this.

She wasn't a psychiatrist, she was just one of my local doctors, but this was the first opportunity she'd had to talk with me alone. This was her first chance, without my Mother being there, to find out exactly what was going on down the road, inside Windrush.

"Anna", she said. "You don't just cut your arms without a reason. My surgery is over in ten minutes. I want you to come home with me and have some tea. Afterwards, I'll drive you back to Windrush."

Once in her car, I felt safe. Jenny instantly behaved more like a friend than a doctor. She was in her late forties, divorced, with two children away at boarding school. Jenny lived in a large cosy two-storey house, overlooking the Helford River, about ten minutes from the surgery. Arriving at her house, we entered her kitchen and sat down at a huge wooden table. In the corner of the kitchen there was a large cage which housed an African grey parrot. Every now and then, in a very loud voice, the parrot would shout:

"Fuck off! Fuck off!"

It was all the parrot could ever say.

I'll never know why but the floodgates burst open and my life's story flowed out. I talked non-stop for nearly three hours without interruption. Sometimes I cried, as I spoke about the most painful parts of my childhood, but even though I wept, I kept talking. While my tears dried, I continued talking until eventually, still talking, I began crying again. Even the parrot seemed to recognise the significance of my words and remained silent as my uncensored, horrific true-life story was told.

I described everything in explicit detail. I was now telling someone how my Grandmother had cruelly inflicted so much torment on me. The huge meals forced down my throat. Being abandoned in Hamleys. The nights spent locked away in the pitch black. Bath times when I was made to stand naked in front of a mirror.

"Fat children grow into fat adults!"
The Sunday tea times when she repeatedly whispered in my ear I'd never have a boyfriend. How I would always fail at school. Years of relentless indoctrination, convincing me I was fat and useless. The sad tale went on and on.

Three hours later, this terrible story finished. Jenny comforted me, then asked many questions, probing even deeper to discover every last detail.

The truth was out.

Then and there, Jenny rang my parents to arrange an appointment for the following lunch time. Her exact words to my Mother and Father were:
"There is something very important your daughter needs to discuss with you both. I would like Anna to do this, with my assistance, tomorrow at 12.00."

"I can't tell them, I can't", I cried to Jenny, as she put the phone down.

"You are going to have to tell them if you're to get better", Jenny replied, holding my hand.

"But my Mother loves Gran and my Father loves Mum", I said. "They won't believe me."

"Listen to me carefully Anna", Jenny began. "At this stage it doesn't matter whether your Mother loves your Grandmother or if your Father is scared of your Gran. We have to address the truth. Your parents have to face facts. However much it hurts them, they are adults and must accept responsibility for allowing your Grandmother to verbally abuse you from such a young age. We'll probably never know exactly how much they knew about it all, but one thing is certain. They cannot bury their heads in the sand any more."

I put on my coat and then, as we were leaving, the parrot shouted:

"Fuck off!"

Will my parents say that to Gran, I thought to myself, when they hear of my misery or will they just say:
"Anna, how could you make up such a pack of lies"?

I'd always so desperately wanted my parents to love me. I was anorexic because of the love I didn't have. My Father screaming about the blocked drains, my Mother complaining about the two hundred-mile trips to visit me in hospital, the four days alone during my brother's wedding and my parents' behaviour towards me for many years.

Which side of the fence would Mum and Dad come down on now?

An hour later, Jenny dropped me off at Windrush. As the car pulled into the drive, my Mother rushed out of the house, trying to talk with Dr Jenny. Sensing a confrontation, Dr Jenny drove off before Mum could say a word.

Inside the bungalow, my parents launched into a full-scale inquisition.

"What is this meeting all about? What are you going to tell us? What's going on?"

I was too tired to even answer and collapsed into my chair in the lounge. My day had been so traumatic. All I wanted to do now was write to my Simon and tell him everything.

"Is it something we've done?" my parents continued.
"Did you tell her about John Denver?" Mum asked, with a funny look on her face.
"Anna come on, tell us. You must tell us what you've said!" chimed in Dad.

They continued to fire questions at me non-stop. My parents were behaving as if they'd been exposed for a crime they'd committed years ago, which they thought they'd got away with. Frustrated that I wouldn't give them any answers, eventually Mum and Dad gave up and went to bed.

I hardly slept at all that night. The idea of having to tell my parents what really happened in Gran's bungalow for all those years was overwhelming.

The voice returned, taunting me.

"Cut yourself! Cut yourself!" it screamed.

"You're going to ruin the lives of your parents. Call yourself a daughter? You're hateful. Cut yourself now!"

Without reprieve, the anorexic voice continued for hours.

"There's no one who cares for you. No one who will mind if you shred yourself to pieces. Go on, cut yourself again!"

"Oh yes there is", I screamed back at the voice.

"There's my Simon, and Simon cares, so you can shut up."

I collected all the blades, carefully wrapping them, writing across the top:
"Handle with great care, these blades are very sharp. Please be careful not to cut yourself."
I put the blades in the envelope to Simon and now I was free.

Free to write my letter to my Simon.

"Dear Simon,

I have never before turned to anyone in an hour of need, as I turn to you now. I trust you so much. Inside my head, there is always a voice. I think it is Gran's voice. The voice always told me not to eat and now, alone in my bedroom, the voice is telling me to cut myself. Instead, I am writing and confiding in you. In cutting my arm, I would be hurting you too and I couldn't bear that. I am posting you the blades for you to throw away. Simon, I know you can help me never to cut myself again."

I ended the letter by explaining in detail the traumatic experience that afternoon at Dr Jenny's house.

Finally, in the early hours of the morning, I got into bed. I
started to dream. I saw myself dressed in black, standing
against a plain white backdrop. Gran, Mark, Tim Wilson
and all the other characters from my past kept coming
into this plain white room to talk to me. As each visitor
arrived, I became thinner and thinner. The unhappiness I
endured in re-meeting these people was only eased by the
knowledge that I was about to vanish. In the dream I was
5 stones, 4 stones, 3 stones, 2 stones, 1 stone. My time
was running out.

I awoke in a cold sweat, my bed drenched, my hair
soaking. I looked at the clock. It was already 6.30 am.
Less than six hours before my parents would finally
know the whole truth.

It seemed only seconds later that we were all sitting in the
lounge - my Mother, Father, Dr Jenny and me.

The most important family meeting of our lives was
about to begin.

Dr Jenny spoke first.
"Mr and Mrs Paterson, please understand it is very
important you do not interrupt Anna while she talks. I
want you both to listen very carefully to her story."

Turning to me, Dr Jenny then said:
"Anna please tell them everything you told me
yesterday."

At first I couldn't speak but then with Dr Jenny carefully
prompting me, the whole sordid story was told. As I
spoke, I sobbed and sobbed, but Dr Jenny made sure I

finished without interruption. My parents sat there, dumbfounded. When I had finished talking, my Mother, as usual, spoke first. She said:

"How could all this have happened to Anna without us knowing about it?"

She then started talking about her own childhood, relating an experience all about bacon.

As a child, her Mother had asked her to buy some bacon from the local shop. The shopkeeper, seeing she was a young child, had cheated and given her the large fatty lump at the end of the joint. He then demanded more money than Mum was given. Paying out of her own pocket money rather than face Gran's wrath, Mum had grabbed the bacon and run home. At home, Gran had complained because the bacon was just one thick fatty slice.

As she was in the middle of repeating this old familiar tale, Dr Jenny interrupted.

"I realise your Mother treated you unkindly too and we will talk about that later but not now. Today, we are here to talk about your daughter Anna. We need to discuss why she cuts her arms and why she tries to starve herself to death."

My Dad, totally silent since the start of the meeting, suddenly spoke.

"That bloody woman!"

Turning to my Mum, he continued.

"Your Mother has ruined our daughter's life - in fact ruined all our lives. How can you go on about bacon again after what Anna's just said to us?"

Everybody seemed to be arguing now about my Mother's bacon, while I just sat there silently. I watched them all blankly, as if I was watching the whole thing on a television programme.

Suddenly Dr Jenny took charge.

"The only way Anna will ever get better is if you now sever all relations with her Grandmother. You have to stop the old lady ringing and certainly stop seeing her altogether. I believe Anna has today told us the whole truth. I emphatically believe it was the Grandmother who sewed the seeds of Anorexia nervosa in your daughter's mind. Anna is your child. You both owe it to her now to help her get well again. You have to cut ties with this sick old woman for good and you have to do it today."

The room suddenly went totally silent. My Mother looked shocked. It was as if an enormous "BUT" was printed across her forehead.

Dr Jenny was again first to speak.

"I am now going to ask you a very important question", Jenny continued. "Think carefully before you answer. Are you prepared to sever all relations with this old lady?"
Dad immediately replied with a very definite "Yes" but Mum started to mumble excuses.
"What if our Grandmother isn't well? She's old now. The shock of all this could kill her."

"I doubt if anything will ever kill the old woman", Jenny muttered. "But we're not talking about her right now. We are talking about Anna, your daughter's health."

"We must of course put Anna first but..." Mum began again.
Before she could give another excuse, Jenny interrupted, speaking very sternly.
"You need to take action now Mrs Paterson for your daughter's sake. Are you prepared to stop seeing your Mother? You could start by never speaking to her on the phone again. Why don't you buy an answerphone?" Jenny suggested.

"We'll do that right away", Dad replied.

"Is that agreed then?" said Jenny, turning to Mum.
"Well I'll try", my Mother replied.
"Try what?" said Dr Jenny, getting really annoyed now.
"Your daughter is seriously ill."

Suddenly Mum stood up and, in front of us all, passed out on the floor. Dad and I just watched in amazement, as Jenny attended her in a medical fashion.
"This is just traumatic shock. Come on Mrs Paterson, let's sit you up now. You don't need mouth to mouth resuscitation", said Jenny, getting increasingly exasperated.

The doctor pulled my Mother back to the chair, as my Father just shook his head in disbelief at his wife's behaviour. With Mum conscious again, the meeting ended with an agreement that we'd buy an answering machine to screen all calls. Dr Jenny left, saying she would return to discuss things further the next day.

I went into my room and broke down in tears. I'd just poured my heart out to my parents, telling them my most deep-rooted secret, yet Mum was still trying to side with my Grandmother.

After all I'd told them, she still worried about Gran's health. Why couldn't she put me, Anna, her daughter, first just this once?

Couldn't my Mother love me enough to put me before Gran?

Couldn't my Father love me enough to put his foot down, even if it meant going against his wife?

The hurt I was feeling was the same hurt that had driven me to cut my arms. The hurt I felt was the same hurt that had driven me to anorexia.

We all need to feel love.

I wanted my Mum and Dad to love me so much but the reassurance I needed so desperately that day, was denied me.

I realised I had nobody.

"Oh no", I screamed at the top of my voice.

"I've got my Simon. My Simon."

Chapter 20

THE VOICE ON THE PHONE

The phone rang.

It was Simon calling. In my last letter to Simon, I'd given him my phone number, hoping he would call so that we could talk all about my confession to Jenny. He'd been away for a few days and had just returned late that evening to find all my letters, including the one containing the blades. He called me immediately.

Four days had passed and so much had happened after I'd posted him the blades, that at first, I couldn't understand the panic in his voice.

"Are you okay? Are you okay?" Simon kept asking.

Simon was so kind and made me promise not to ever harm myself again. He also made me swear that we would talk every day on the phone.

"What looks so black now will seem like nothing in a couple of month's time. Anna, I've got a wonderful surprise for you", Simon proudly announced. "I've got tickets for an REM concert."
Simon already knew that REM were my favourite pop group.

I couldn't believe how my life was changing. 24 hours previously I had been in the depths of despair and now look at me. I was talking on the phone to a man who cared about me and was taking me to a concert to see my favourite band.

The phone call lasted for two hours and at midnight, I felt safe and went to sleep peacefully for the first time in years.

The day after Simon's call, I felt as though I was walking on air. I was actually living my own real life for the first time. I wanted to speak to him again immediately but I was afraid he hadn't liked me. What if he thought I was silly and childish?

I had Simon's number now but I was too scared to ring him. All day, I kept picking up the phone, dialling all but the last digit, only to put the receiver down each time, still too afraid to speak. That afternoon I wrote to him instead, asking him what he'd thought of me.

Simon's reply was very reassuring for me but it highlighted his own insecurity. He told me how much he had loved talking with me and how excited he was that he'd actually been able to get us tickets for the REM concert in June. As always, our similar characteristics were obvious. He was worried I hadn't liked him and put himself down.
"Do you think you'll be able to put up with me for the whole evening of the concert?" he apprehensively wrote.

Simon was also very annoyed with my Grandmother. He wanted to kill her. Why weren't my parents doing as Dr Jenny had suggested, cutting off all ties with her completely? Simon said I should challenge my parents and insist they never see Gran again.

I wanted so much to do as Simon suggested but I couldn't confront my parents. My Mother cared more for Gran than she did for me, so why would she do as I asked? The next day, I showed Simon's letter to Dr Jenny and she agreed wholeheartedly with him. At our next family meeting, Jenny brought up the subject of Gran again. My Grandmother had in fact contacted us many times during that week. She'd left messages on the new answerphone, asking to speak to me. I now jumped every time the phone rang.

"Kay, it's only me, your Mother. I just want to speak to Anna. Is she there? Anna, Anna are you there dear?"

Her voice echoed round the bungalow, as if she was actually there, sending shivers up and down my spine.

The next time we all sat down for therapy, it seemed like Simon was sitting in the room next to me, as Jenny showed my parents his letter.

"Simon suggests what?" said my Mother.

"He suggested we don't see your Mother any more", my Dad replied.

"Who's suggesting what?" repeated my Mother.

"Simon's suggesting", said Dad.

"Simon who?" said Mum.

"My Simon", I said, feeling proud for the first time ever.

"I'm going to write a letter", said my Dad. "A letter to that woman."
My Father looked me in the eyes and said:
"I'm going to write your Grandmother a letter and tell her what I should have said 20 years ago."

My Dad now wrote the letter of his life, which read as follows:

"Dear Vera,

I have always believed we are able to control the way we behave, but am informed people suffering from personality disorders cannot. Perhaps your attitude to us, your son Ron, your daughter Kay, your grandsons, your granddaughter Anna, your great grandson and your in-laws should be explained in these terms. Your daughter Kay and I always tried to meet your aggression with kindness. Despite your apparent belief money is the key to everything and people could be bought, we took you on holidays and entertained you every Sunday afternoon and evening, because we wanted to look after you.

I have never been able to understand your contempt for your own children, particularly Kay, who I have loved deeply for nearly forty years, but failed to protect. I learnt early in our marriage, that if I took you to task over your actions, you waited until I was at work and then punished her. I thought moving across town would give us more breathing space but I was wrong. You moved too and strengthened your grip. Later, your desire to have Uncle Reg's estate nearly cost Kay her sanity.

To my own shame I failed to support Ron, when he wrote to you about the problems with his own mental health and the part you played. Ron no more deserved your displeasure than Kay. He is a highly intelligent, likeable and hard working man who has our respect and our love.

I suppose it was through ignorance that we failed to see your affect on our daughter Anna. Why did you deliberately rob her of her self-esteem? Was it because she was pretty and intelligent or was it just that she was a little girl? For the life of me, I cannot understand anyone who mentally abuses children, both their own and others. It has taken thousands of hours of therapy to start to remove the barriers you placed in her mind, to stop her telling us about what you were doing to her through all those years. All those hateful things you said that we had said about her, when we had trusted you, her Grandmother, with her care. All those awful things you did to a little girl. Was your letter to her in hospital, telling her that her Mother and Father no longer wanted her, a final attempt to silence her? It nearly succeeded. When we arrived in Cornwall, our bright and beautiful daughter was dying. Every morning, for months on end, we got up and expected her to be dead.

For many years we have acted out a charade. If no one tells the truth about our situation, perhaps we will survive. But we have been hurt just the same, at times almost mortally. If you had given yourself over to be a loving Mother, Mother-in-law and Grandmother, you would be living with us now, and it would have given us so much joy.

We are unable to continue to take punishment and we refuse to turn our meetings with you, either in person or on the telephone, into slanging matches. Your present desire, to bring everything out into the open, leaves us with only one direction. To continue making a life for ourselves, improving its quality, we have to break contact.

I will send duplicates of this letter to everyone in the family. They have the right to know I have finally found the courage to place on record the way I feel.

With due care,

Your son-in-law Mike Paterson"

When Dad showed me this letter, I sobbed as I read it. My Father, who had never had the courage to stand up to Gran or my Mother, had found his moment of truth. For all my Father's shortcomings, what Dad had just done meant a great deal to me. My Father had written the letter, which hadn't been easy to write. It was, for him, a very important thing to do. My Father had shown me he did care and how I was important to him.

It took me a lot of courage but I did ring Simon to tell him everything that had happened. The answerphone kicked in and my heart sank. I wanted so much to speak to my Simon and all I was getting was a recorded message.

I began to leave a message, when suddenly I heard a crash, a frantic scrabbling and a breathless:
"Anna? Anna? Is that you?"
His phone ringer had been accidentally switched off and all Simon heard was his answerphone machine, was my voice filling his room. Already in love with me, he had fallen over his chair, diving across the room to pick up the phone. We had a wonderful four hour conversation and for the first time I realised I was falling in love with this kind, shy and funny man.

Now as well as writing three or four letters daily to each other, we were on the phone every other hour.

By that Friday, I wasn't falling any more. I was deeply in love with Simon.

I wrote him a letter, clumsily telling him how much he meant to me.

"Dear Simon,

This is very hard for me to say but I have not felt the way I feel for you, ever before in my life. You are incredibly special to me and I care about you so much. I don't think you will want to hear that I love you though, because nobody could ever love me in return."

As soon as I'd posted the letter I regretted it. Simon would never feel the same way. I'd ruined our friendship. He'd now think I was pushy and forward, would feel pressured and probably stop writing. I considered sitting by the post box, waiting for the postman to arrive, to ask for my letter back. But it was Saturday night and it would be too long a wait until the postman came on Monday morning.

When Simon phoned late that evening, I sounded subdued and he asked me why. For half an hour I dodged his questions but eventually I told him what was upsetting me.

"This afternoon I sent you a letter telling you how much I care about you and I'm worried", I sheepishly said.

"How much do you care about me?" Simon asked me.

"A lot", I replied.

"How much is a lot?" was his next question.

For twenty minutes, we verbally danced around the subject, without actually speaking honestly.

Finally, after taking a deep breath, I almost shouted at Simon:

"I love you, okay?"

There was silence at the other end of the phone, then Simon said:

"Say that last bit again."

"I love you", I repeated.

"And I love you too", Simon replied.

The romance was officially on.

Our conversation that night went on for another five hours and we constantly talked of our love for each other.

Several months later, I found out Simon had actually fallen in love with me by the time he received my third letter.

By now we were desperate to meet. By chance, more fortune was with us. My parents had, for some time, planned a visit to Southend in April. We were all going to stay with my brother, and this was an ideal opportunity to come down from Cornwall and meet Simon. I talked it all over with Simon and we agreed to see each other. Now Simon and I had committed ourselves and made the arrangement to meet, our nerves began. Mum and Dad were spending three days with my brother, so this gave Simon and I not one day to meet, but three.

Simon and I excitedly discussed what we would do on each of these three different visits, on consecutive days out.

As the time approached, we talked incessantly on the phone. It was quite funny really. We hadn't even met yet but we were behaving like an old married couple. I'd often joke with Simon about him always wearing black. He never wore any other colour. I'd even sent him the Will Smith record "Men In Black". Simon dressing in black was his way of hiding from the world in just the same way as I had worn baggy clothes. One day Simon rang me, very excited, telling me about the new blue shirt he'd bought.

"I've never bought a coloured shirt in my life before", he laughed.

I smiled to myself as I told him what I'd be wearing. It was so wonderful. For the first time ever, I wanted to look really special for someone. Choosing clothes was still difficult because, even though I was matchstick thin, I couldn't see this. In my anorexic eyes, I still looked fat in everything I tried on. It took me weeks to decide which three outfits I would take with me to wear when I saw Simon.

As the big day approached, both Simon and I grew increasingly nervous. Strangely, a few days before we met, a calm seemed to descend upon Simon. While I called him, in tears on many occasions, talking about my fears, he kept repeating that everything would be all right.

"We love each other don't we?" he kept saying to me.

"Yes", I replied.

"Well we're going to be alright, I'm telling you", he kept assuring me.

Early that Wednesday morning, I got in the car with my parents and we all travelled down to Southend. The following morning, my parents dropped me at Southend railway station, where I caught a train to meet Simon in London.

The moment had come. I was unbelievably edgy but so excited. I could hear my heart beating.

For our first special day, I was dressed in a new pair of blue leggings and a brightly coloured yellow shirt. The weather that morning was so cold, I had to cover all my beautiful new clothes with a coat. I laughed inwardly to myself on the train, thinking this is ridiculous. You keep looking at yourself in the mirror, checking you look nice and presentable. You're in love. It was a miracle. Looking in the toilet mirror momentarily, I looked beautiful.

Not fat but beautiful.

That's the power of love.

I wondered if Simon would be brave enough to wear the new coloured shirts he'd bought for the occasion.

This was the first time in thirteen years I'd travelled by train on my own. Locked in my anorexic prison, all I'd ever thought about, talked about or dreamed about for years was Mum, Dad, Gran and food. Now although still painfully thin, weighing around 7 and a half stones (105 lbs.).

I was back in the real world.

No, that wasn't quite true. I wasn't back in the real world. I'd just found it. I'd never been in it before.

I was 30 years old and, due to my anorexia, had not experienced monthly periods for 14 years. This subject was sensitive for me because, only eight weeks previously, I had physically reached womanhood, with my periods being induced by hormone treatments.

Looking out of the train window, I thought back to my hospital bed, being drip-fed in Heath House, all the psychiatrists, all the treatment I'd had.

It had all been a living nightmare.

Sadly, it had all been my life.

I felt so good.

The nightmare was over.

The fairytale was about to begin.

No, not about to begin. It had already started. I was in the middle of it.

I was travelling on a train to meet my boyfriend, Simon, and we were going out, like other ordinary couples, for the day together.

I wasn't being checked into some psychiatric ward.

I wasn't standing on the weighing scales, with my pockets full of stones.

I wasn't flushing food down the toilet.

I was on my way to meet Simon.

How would I handle seeing him?

What would happen between us?

Would he try and kiss me?

I wondered if we would go as far as making love? We'd already discussed on the phone our lack of sexual experience and knew that we'd have to take everything very slowly, but would we? How slow is "slowly"?

I hadn't kissed a man before and I tried to imagine how it would feel.

Was Simon thinking similar thoughts to me at that precise moment?

It really was amazing we'd ever come together. Here we were; two people from the opposite sides of Britain, who'd spent most of their lives hiding from life. Now fate had brought us together. We had found the courage to enter into real life and face love, with all it's difficulties and drawbacks. Isolated in our bedrooms, we couldn't get hurt by lovers. No one could be indifferent or cruel to us, let alone abandon us.

To find life, to find love, we had to take risks and that's what we both were doing. Was Simon my escape from the world of misery and anorexia, into the world of health and happiness?

Had it all been written years before, in the Book of Time? If so, I smiled.

"Where will this fairytale end?"

THE MAN IN BLACK SPEAKS

Chapter 21

THE MAN IN BLACK

Finally the train reached Fenchurch Street Station, and with my knees trembling, I started to rehearse my "Hello". After leaving the train, I looked around the station and panicked. I couldn't see Simon anywhere. Why wasn't he there? Was it all just a dream? I sat down, half expecting my Grandmother to appear and say:

"I told you Anna. I told you you'd never get a boyfriend."

Suddenly I looked up and saw somebody rushing towards me.

My man in black.

The only colour I could see was two beige shirt collars, sticking up at strange angles beneath his jumper. This had to be Simon. I smiled, seeing he was already apologising before he'd even reached me. Watching him cross the station, I was overcome with shyness. I couldn't even look him in the eyes and just stared down at my feet, unable to speak. Simon looked just like his photos. He had dark curly hair, a wonderful smile and a kind face. He was well spoken and clearly an intelligent man. I wanted to impress him and say something clever but all I could do was stupidly giggle constantly. We were both so awkward. I'd imagined a serenely calm meeting when I would hug Simon and he would kiss me. I had not expected this shy, embarrassed teenage meeting. We couldn't even touch one another.

Here we were, aged 30, like two kids of twelve, too embarrassingly shy to even speak to one another. It's a wonder we didn't run away then and there.

"Science Museum", Simon blurted out, nervously looking up.
"Science Museum?" I asked.
"Well that's where we agreed to go", Simon nervously said.
And the world's biggest romance story began, walking around London's Science Museum. Neither of us were remotely interested in any of the exhibits, and for the next hour, hardly spoke a word until we accidentally walked into the hall of mirrors and weighing scales. We turned, looked at each other in horror, and scuttled out.

It was lunch time and Simon nervously said:
"Shall we go and eat then?"
We left the Science Museum and found ourselves standing outside the main gates in the busy Cromwell Road, when Simon spoke again.
"You choose the restaurant because I'm totally useless at choosing anything. In fact I'm just totally useless."
"Stop it", I shouted. "I hate it when you belittle yourself."

Suddenly, for one brief moment in time, the world stopped spinning round and I reached out and took his hand.

Without knowing it, we'd thrown each other the lifeline we needed. Grabbing that lifeline, he grasped my hand and didn't let go.

Now we were off together to find a café, walking through the back streets of Kensington.

I felt wonderful!

We felt wonderful!

Everything was wonderful!

This was how life was meant to be. Happily walking along hand in hand with the man I loved. The initial awkwardness now had vanished, and for that moment, love had taken over.

We soon found a small restaurant. Simon still held me tight, gripping my hand, and there was no way he was ever going to let go. It took ages for us to be served and suddenly, overcoming his shyness, Simon started to tell me about himself.

"I've always been very shy", he said.

"You don't seem shy to me", I replied.

"I'm not, I don't feel shy with you", he continued. "I've never had a proper girlfriend but with you I feel wonderful."

The soup then came and interrupted his speech. With just one hand, I drank as much as I could and then our meal arrived, which was more difficult to eat. Still Simon held my hand tightly under the table, looking at me with the sweetest grin on his face, telling me he loved me. I giggled in response.

Three times Simon nervously repeated himself, saying:
"I love you. I love you. I love you."
The meal continued with me giggling. Simon spilled food
down his jumper and me, trying so desperately to eat
normally, dropped beans all over my lap. With our hands
still locked together, we stood up and for the next few
hours, we walked through the shops and around the
parks, just talking. Walking side by side, we couldn't talk
face to face. In a way, not looking at each other, it was
like we were still on the phone but it felt comfortable and
for the two of us, it was a start.

By late afternoon I desperately needed a rest and, still
holding hands, we ventured into a bookshop. Each with
one hand free, we tried to act in an adult manner glancing
through various books. Selecting the latest paperbacks
was quite amusing really. We were trying to choose a
book with one hand and hold hands with the other.

By the time we returned to Fenchurch Street Station, we
had held hands relentlessly for seven hours. Waiting on
the platform, I finally found the courage to look Simon in
the eyes. He looked sad. Was he unhappy being forced to
spend so much time with me? Was he just waiting for the
day to end so he could get away? The insecurity raged on
inside me.

I boarded the train. With the door open and with the train
actually pulling away, we somehow managed to let go of
each other. We had stopped holding hands.

"Do you want to see me again tomorrow?" I called out,
as the train pulled away

"I love you, I want to see you every day", he shouted back.

"Every day for the rest of our lives", he screamed in the distance.

We'd arranged for Simon to meet my parents the following day at Southend Station. I loved him so much by now. I was very proud of Simon and wanted to introduce him to Mum and Dad. The reaction of my parents was not as I so desperately wanted. Mum and Dad, in their usual fashion, had allotted one hour from their busy schedule to meet my first ever boyfriend. Simon's train arrived late and my parents, unwilling to rearrange their important agenda, said a very brief hello and, after giving us both a lift to the centre of town, drove off leaving us alone together.

As soon as their car was out of sight, our hands seemed to automatically reach out for each other. Simon and I stayed with our hands locked together for the rest of that day. Not once did we stop holding hands. For our first romantic hour together, we watched sharks swim up and down in an enormous tank in the Sea Life Centre. We sat on a bench, and instead of gazing into each other eyes, we stared up at those enormous savage fish.
"Look at those beautiful sharks. They are so like the ones I have in my bedroom", said Simon to me in a loving voice.
"Sharks?" I said, looking at him a bit strangely.
"No, I mean furry sharks, toy animals, not real ones", Simon said, giggling.

Any nervous sexual thoughts I might have been trying to summon up that day, soon sunk to the bottom of the tank. Our romantic interlude was soon interrupted by hoards of screaming school children, so we moved on.

Looking at those sharks, I was suddenly hit by the realisation I was in my first serious relationship. I felt very scared. I didn't know what was expected of me.
"Was he going to kiss me or talk about sharks teeth?" I smiled to myself.

Lunch time arrived. With my hand firmly gripped in Simon's, he led me to a seafront café, where we sat down without releasing our grip. I went a la carte and chose beans on toast for my meal. Simon laughed and commenting that beans were in season, ordered the same.
"Tomato-based food is all I ever eat with you", he said jovially, dropping the first of many beans down his T-shirt.
By this time I was feeling much more comfortable with Simon and, giggling loudly, I speared the dropped beans with a fork and ate them.
"You're not going to eat me too", laughed Simon.
At that stage, I just wanted to kiss him on the cheek and, still holding his hand, I leaned over and accidentally tipped the whole plate of beans into his lap. Now we just laughed hysterically, as somehow we managed to clear up the mess, still holding hands.

Like Siamese twins joined at the hands, we left the café and started to walk down the seafront as it began to rain.

"Shall we go and see a film?" Simon suggested.

Thinking Simon would choose a romantic film like "Gone With The Wind" or "The Sound of Music", I faithfully followed him into the cinema. We sat down, but instead of Mary Poppins, it was Mel Gibson in "Payback", ripping out somebody's nose ring. Seeing the blood squirt everywhere, I turned to Simon saying:
"I'm going to vomit. Can we leave please?"

We left the cinema and walked to a park, while Simon talked constantly about films. He was nervous. So was I. We had a coffee in a café and then phoned my parents, who picked us both up ten minutes later. As the white Mondeo came into sight, our vice like grip instantly came apart. I wasn't brave enough yet to let Mum and Dad actually see me holding hands with a man. I was only 30 years old after all.

We dropped Simon off at the station. I felt extremely awkward standing there with my parents, watching as I waved goodbye to Simon as he walked slowly through the barriers. I'd wanted so much to put my arms round him to hug him but with my parents watching, I couldn't pluck up the courage. Simon stood at the barrier, waving endlessly. I felt like a naughty little girl who'd done something wrong, expecting my parents to say to me:
"You didn't kiss him did you?"
I half expected Dad to say:
"He didn't touch you, did he?"

Our third meeting was for the following day, this time, back in London again. Making certain I had a different outfit on, this time I wore red leggings and a blue shirt. I caught the train to London. Looking back, I think because of our nervousness, we'd arranged an extremely busy schedule, like tourists, filling our day with sightseeing events, rather than just allowing ourselves to get to know each other. We went to The Tower of London, wandering around with the sightseers. It had been a very hectic two days for me and by now I was feeling the strain. We went into a small café off Leicester Square. The three dates on the trot, all this normal living, suddenly it was too much for me. I was overcome with exhaustion. The anorexic voice had returned.

"Leave Simon now, never see him again. Go home now!"

"I feel so ill", I said to Simon.

"What's wrong?" Simon softly replied.

"It's me that's wrong. I've always been wrong. I'm no good for you. I'm no good for anyone", I said, crying.

"I can't stay with you any longer. I have to go back to Southend. I have to go now."

"Please stay. Let's go to the cinema", Simon said. "Look, I've already bought the tickets."

"I can't", I replied, suddenly standing up and running from the café.

"Anna! Anna! Come back!" said Simon, catching up with me in the street.
He put his arm round me and said:
"Is it me? Don't you love me any more?"

We held each other tight and cried together.

"Is it me?" Simon repeated.

"No, it's not you at all", I replied. "If only you knew the truth", I sobbed.

"Tell me", pleaded Simon.

"Simon, I love you, but I think so little of myself, I don't know if I can carry on living."

"I love you too", Simon said. "Promise you'll ring me immediately when you get back to Southend."
Like two lost children, we made our way back to Fenchurch Street Station, where I caught the train to Southend.

Later, after I'd arrived back in Southend, I tried desperately to ring Simon. At first, all I got was his answerphone.
"Oh no", I said to myself. "I've ruined it. Why did I have to be ill?"

"Why did I listen to the voice again? Why didn't I just tell it to shut up?"

"Why didn't I just kiss him? I wanted to so much. Why have I wasted so much of my life listening to that voice?"

Our precious day had drifted away. But at least we had finally managed to look each other in the eyes.
God or fate must have brought us together - two of us who were so lost and needed to find love so desperately.

Here were two twelve-year-old children, living in thirty-year-old adult bodies. Both in at the emotional deep end, swimming on trust only. Trust in one another's true love.

Eventually I got through on the phone to Simon and I was shocked but excited when Simon said:
"Anna, next time I see you, I am going to kiss you on the lips."

I was speechless. I'd not kissed anybody in my life. Would I be any good? I wondered were there emergency evening classes in Cornwall for kissing?

"Did you hear me?" Simon said boldly.

"Yes, I did", I replied, rather shyly.

"What did I say?" came back the authoritative voice.

"You said you were going to…"

"Going to what?" came back the impatient, somewhat annoyed reply.

"Kiss me on the lips", I whispered back.

"Okay, I'll see you in three weeks time", Simon said.

"Okay", I replied.

Now both overcome with embarrassment at our lewdness, we rang off before the conversation could go any further.

Two seconds later, the phone rang.

"Oh the lips, I said."

"I know you did", I replied, and put the phone back down.

The following morning, my parents drove me back to Cornwall and late that night, as we opened the front door, there was a letter from Simon he'd written after our first meeting. He didn't think I loved him. Simon was so much like me, it was just unreal. He found it impossible to accept anyone could love him.

"Dear Anna,

Welcome Home. I'm writing this after our first scary meeting. I'm horribly paranoid about what you really think of the 3D me. Please tell me as honestly as you possibly can. Don't spare my feelings. I won't say too much "I love you" stuff because I don't want to pressure you. But you're a lovely person Anna and I really enjoyed meeting up. The ball's in your court, sweetie."

As soon as I read Simon's note, I telephoned him. I told him again how much I loved him. We talked and talked for another six hours about how we could try to handle our nerves better the next time we met.

"When we next meet each other, I'm going to kiss you right on the lips. Remember, we agreed?" Simon said.

To which I replied:

"Yes, and I could kiss you while you are kissing me."

"I think that's how it works", came the voice from down the phone.

Looking back, some of our telephone conversations were hilarious.

"You know I'm going to kiss you on the lips when we meet", Simon whispered, late one night.

"Yeah", I said, very cautiously.

"I'm going to ask you a straight question."

"Yeah?" I replied, even more nervously, practically dropping the phone.

"Can I touch you while we kiss?"

"I suppose so", I blurted out.

"No, I mean, can I unbutton your shirt while we're kissing and put my hand inside?"

"But what happens if I'm wearing a T-shirt with no buttons?" I said, feeling more confident.

Simon started muttering and then blurted out "Well could I just stick my hand up...Oh I gotta go. I'll ring you back in an hour's time. We'll talk about it then."

Exactly an hour later, the phone rang again. It was Simon.

"Hi Anna."

"Hi Simon."

"I just rang to erm I just rang to er erm to er erm ask if you've got the latest REM record?"

"What - REM Unbuttoned?" I giggled.

"No, not your buttons", Simon replied, getting all tongue-tied again.

"Don't forget, I'm going to kiss you on the lips", said Simon.

"I haven't forgotten", I replied.

"It'll all come undone one way or another...I mean all come together one way or another."

How many couples have four hours conversations concerning their feelings about sex? Usually, even the first time, it is totally spontaneous.

Back in Cornwall, I was very excited as I told Dr Jenny every last detail of the three-day visit.
"I suppose I have a boyfriend. I must have", I said with a grin.
"Looks like it", replied Jenny, laughing.
Then and there, in front of me, she phoned Simon.
"Anna, we are going to ring him right away. Give me his number."
"Ring him now?"

I looked at her in surprise.

"You and Simon need to get together again, soon, really soon", she firmly stated. "I'll let you have the top floor of my house for as long as you like", said Jenny, putting her arms around me.

We rang then and there from Jenny's office and Simon and I couldn't refuse this offer from Jenny. We agreed that at the end of May, Simon would come down to Cornwall.

Over the next three weeks, we spoke up to ten times each day, both growing increasingly anxious about this next meeting and that dreaded planned kiss on the lips. Every telephone conversation was like a chess game, trying to check mate each other into saying the words 'kiss' and 'lips'.

I was very excited in many ways on the evening Simon arrived, once again, dressed in black. After checking into Dr Jenny's house we decided we wanted some time on our own.

We had something to do!

Ready for action, we went for a walk along a deserted cliff top. Sitting just above Helston Creek, overlooking the sparkling crystal clear water which was covered in boats. Simon leaned over and asked:

"Shall I do it now?"

"Do what?" I asked.

"Kiss you on the lips", Simon replied, sheepishly.

"No, no not here", I said. "People can still see us. Over there, by that tree", I replied.

My heart was now pounding.

"Oh no, what have I agreed to?" I thought to myself.

Reaching the first tree, Simon leaned over and said "What, here?"

"No, no, no, not this tree", I replied. "Over there a bit more, by that tree."

"Which tree?" said Simon, getting annoyed.

"I'll show you the tree in a minute", I said.

Going over the top of the hill, Simon breathlessly turned to me with a strained look on his face.

"Anna", he said, peering down the hill. "There are no more trees."

"I know, but come on. There's a big bush down there. Will that do?" I said, dragging him down the other side.

"Tree, bush, does it matter?" said Simon, turning me around.

Before I knew it, I was being kissed for the first time in my whole life.

We were at first very nervous but, once started, began to make up for lost time.

Later that evening we returned to Jenny's, who acted like a Victorian schoolmistress, showing us to our separate respective bedrooms and closing the doors behind us. We were the only ones on the top floor, and from about 10.00 pm that evening, behind closed doors, we called out to each other.

"I love you Anna", Simon softly called.

"What did you say?" I replied.

"I said I love you", Simon yelled back at the top of his voice.

This went on for quite a while, until Jenny eventually came upstairs.
"Come on you two lovebirds, we have got to get some sleep in this house. This is ridiculous. Leave all this to the morning and keep those doors closed", she said, walking down the stairs.

The next day we went walking outside the village I lived in, stopping every ten yards for another kiss along the way. We eventually got tired and sat down, where we carried on kissing in the midday sunshine. An hour and a half later we surfaced, both badly sunburnt on one side of our faces only.

The whole four days were magical - one long Cornish kiss.

Simon and I still felt really shy around each other physically, as both of us were self-conscious about our bodies. I was still very nervous about being naked in front of anyone. I hated my body and was ashamed of the way I looked. Simon helped me as much as he could, with constant reassurance.

"You really are beautiful Anna. I love you. You should never be ashamed of how you look", Simon said, giving me another kiss.

He himself was also painfully shy and I felt honoured as I could feel him growing more comfortable around me. Being with each other, it felt like our inhibitions were falling away like layers of an onion being peeled. As each layer came off, we were both meeting each other and ourselves for the very first time.

On the last morning, I drove Simon to the station. Holding hands, we waited nervously for his train to arrive. We both wanted to cry but for each other's sake acted bravely. Simon climbed aboard the train and I was just about to start waving goodbye when he jumped back off, saying:

"Oh God, I forgot. I wanted to ask you something."

With that, he got down on one knee, on the platform and held out a small jewellery box, and said...

Nothing. Not a word. He just knelt there, holding out this box.

There was an announcement on the station tannoy.

"The train from Platform 3 will be departing in three minutes."

The next three minutes were the longest of our lives as I just stared at Simon kneeling below me on the floor. He didn't say a word and I couldn't say a word.

A whistle went.

"Will you?" he blurted out, taking my hand.

"Yes, I will", I replied, as he put the ring on my finger.

As Simon leapt on the train, he shouted above the noise:

"Really? Really? Do you mean it? Do you mean it? Will you?"

"Definitely", I said, waving goodbye to him as the train pulled out of sight.

With the train long gone, I went back to the station buffet and reflected on my life. I looked down at my ring and thought my fairy tale has just come true. I was missing Simon already, I was so glad that this was the man I was going to spend the rest of my life with.

A month later, after 54 million phone calls and 28 million letters, we met for the REM concert.

I couldn't believe how my life was unfolding. The evening was magical. We had an early supper by candlelight in an Italian restaurant and then made our way to Earls Court for the REM concert.

Watching REM performing for two hours was amazing. They played many of my favourite songs but it was still "Everybody Hurts" that affected me most. As the first note started, I was transported back to the Drama Therapy room at Heath House Hospital, with the occupational therapist telling me:

"Allow yourself to feel Anna. You'll never be truly free until you can admit how much you hurt."

With the tears running down my face, I realised how far I'd come since I'd met Simon. I now ate foods I'd never dreamed of having before, such as chips and chocolate. I went out for the evening to the cinema and concerts and travelled around the country like other normal adult human beings. I wasn't just a label or hospital number any longer - 'An Anorexic Girl.' Everybody looked at me now as a normal person, and when men looked at me, I didn't see pity in their eyes the way I always had before. They looked at me like they were attracted to me.

Anorexia had stolen my early life but now my time had come. I was fighting back.

I heard Michael Stipe sing the words:

"If you think you've had too much of this life, well hold on."

I had held on. Only just, but I'd managed to survive. Looking down at my hand with the new engagement ring, I smiled. My life was still very hard. There were many unresolved problems in my mind but I was starting to heal. The song came to an end and Simon turned to me.

He had a look of concern on his face as he saw the tears. I smiled reassuringly at him. For the first time in my life I felt a strong sexual desire. I wanted to throw away my inhibitions. I felt so lucky to have found Simon. I wanted this night to go on forever.

Leaving the REM concert, we went home to an empty house. We were a couple overcoming a lifetime of fears, a lifetime of insecurities. We both knew we wanted to but could we take that final leap and make love?

Simon had patiently waited until I was ready for this special moment. Up until this night I had felt so afraid. I had known the mechanics of sex and exactly where everything was supposed to go since I was twelve but I was petrified. Simon and I were both still virgins, which was very unusual for two people aged 30. But then we had both led very unusual and sheltered lives.

We held each other tight and love took over. Very soon, we were both naked in each other's arms, as if our pasts had never happened.

That evening, everything was so different. Our emotions were already running high. My nerves had gone. I was allowing Simon to completely see the body of which I felt so ashamed. I felt comfortable naked and I could see Simon did too. His gentle touch sent shivers down my spine. This wasn't mad passionate erotic sex, it was a gentle tender lovemaking. Simon's caresses were so light, my body reacted with goose bumps and all the hairs on my arms stood on end. The evening was hot and gently Simon blew on my face to cool me. As we came together, our two bodies joined to form one and it felt as though we were floating. I loved Simon so much. I couldn't understand why I'd been so afraid of this moment. I could see the desire in Simon's eyes when he looked at me. I had to learn to trust him when he told me I was beautiful. I had to try to learn to love my body the way that he did.

Lying in each other's arms, a freedom came over me like I'd never felt before. We talked about what we'd do the next day. We romanticised about our future - where we would live, what we would do.

We kissed each other and made love again.

My life had just begun.

Anna was in love. Anna was alive.

For me there were many more hills to climb. Steep, steep hills. Anorexic type hills. Inch by inch, day by day, I climbed them. There are good days and bad days but I am never going back to the voice.

A day at a time, for today I've beaten anorexia and with that spirit, I'll face tomorrow when it comes.

Thank you for reading my story.

SIMON AND ANNA

TOURING THE U.K.

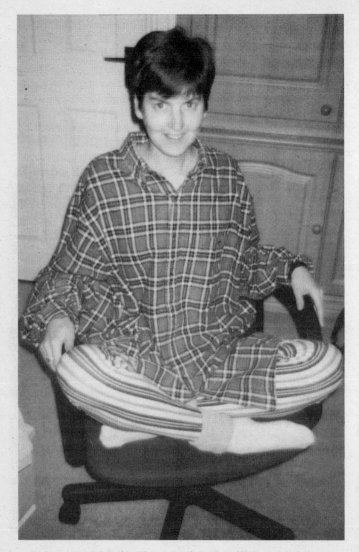

A NEW CHAIR TO SIT ON

RETURN TO HAMELYS TOY STORE

ANNA DOING BUSINESS

Knowing Anna
by Simon Teff

Before Anna, my life had settled into a rut. In my 20s, I gradually lost confidence in ever having a relationship with a woman. My lack of self-confidence meant I'd given up trying to even find a girlfriend.

I spent most of my time in the upstairs bedroom of my parents' house, watching films and listening to music. I often slept all day because I had no reason to be awake. The music reviews I did for a magazine I co-owned didn't require strict working hours. I drifted aimlessly and often only realised it was a new month when the next TV listings magazine arrived.

When I wrote to Anna, my expectations weren't high. I was expecting a pen friend and nothing more. Her first letter was sweet, funny and very direct and I replied immediately.

Anna's directness and honesty led me to open up in a way I never had before. When Anna told me she suffered with Anorexia nervosa, I felt privileged that she had trusted me so much. To me though, Anna, even at that stage, was already more than just a friend. I was falling in love for the first time ever.

After the fifth letter, I thought I'd blown it when Anna wrote a letter calling herself a "revolting fat pig" and I responded, saying that I found her comment offensive. I am overweight myself and I also got upset on behalf of all overweight people everywhere.

I realised I'd made a mistake as soon as I got Anna's wounded response. I felt terrible and suddenly found myself at a newsagent buying handfuls of "Sorry" cards.

Anna's letters soon became the most important part of my life. The arrival of the post each morning was the highlight of my day.

Anna wrote to me late one night saying she'd had a bad day. She'd been about to cut herself, but had written to me, sending the blades through the post instead. I was shocked but I felt proud and amazed that, through my friendship, I'd been able to prevent Anna from seriously injuring herself. Because I was away when the letter with the blades arrived, I received everything two days late but finding the blades, rang her immediately. By this time thankfully Anna had recovered and over the phone sounded much quieter than I expected.

That night, I was very nervous on the phone and began to babble, with Anna only giving a brief reply to each question. I felt awkward and was running out of conversation, when Anna suddenly said:
"I think you should go now".
It was my first experience of Anna's extremely dry sense of humour. I thought she was serious and was convinced I'd screwed up. But then I heard a giggle and we both began to relax and enjoy the conversation.

Once the ice had been broken, Anna started to open up and tell me how she was really feeling. I then surprised her by telling her I had managed to get two tickets for an REM concert. I thought Anna would be excited when I told her the news but instead she just seemed upset. I was certain this was because she didn't want to spend a whole evening with me but then she said:

"I'm sorry Simon, I can't go with you. I don't deserve to see REM."

I was very upset to see that she could think so little of herself but after much persuasion, I managed to convince her to come along with me.

After that first shaky conversation, our phone calls became more frequent. We had as many as ten some days and others lasted for up to five hours at a time. We also continued to write letters daily. Before long, we knew each another inside and out. I will never know when the phone calls crossed the line between friendship and romance but they did.

I couldn't believe it when Anna told me that she loved me. I'd always been scared and cynical about the "L" word as I had seen so many relationships go wrong around me. I'd never told anyone I loved them to their face before but I had no difficulty in telling Anna. I was buzzing with happiness after the call and went to post her a card. I didn't notice it was 4 am or that a gale was blowing the dustbins around on the high street. All I could think about was Anna and worry about whether her feelings would change when we met.

Anna suggested we meet up and as the day approached, I became increasingly frightened and unsure of myself. When I met Anna she was even prettier than in her photos - tall and slender with big blue eyes and a shy smile. We were meeting for the first time as girlfriend and boyfriend. How should I behave? I raised my arms slightly to hug her, but she didn't notice and we stood there awkwardly. We went to the Science Museum as planned but neither of us was really interested in "The Oldest Tin Can In History". We shuffled around, too embarrassed to even look at one another properly.

Anna was so pretty, and on our first date, I felt certain that she was way out of my league. I thought she'd lost interest and was now just humouring me. I kept up a cheery front as best I could but inside I felt as though a part of me was dying.

During our third meeting Anna finally told me she loved me and it felt wonderful but as soon as we parted I began to wonder if I had imagined her words, and then started to worry she'd change her mind.

Within minutes of her train leaving, I sent Anna a card saying I still loved her but would understand if she didn't feel the same way. My question was answered before she even received the card, when later that day she phoned to say she missed me already. I felt incredibly relieved.

Our next meeting was a few weeks later in Cornwall.

Anna met me at the station. Later we both wandered down to a deserted beach, where we walked hand in hand for an hour and, under my leadership, we were soon lost. We sat down on a deserted clifftop facing the sea and I asked her if I could have my kiss now. The next few days were wonderful.

I had wanted to ask Anna to marry me for weeks now and had brought an engagement ring with me. I was in Cornwall for four days during which all day everyday I tried to say, "Anna will you marry me?" but I could not say anything. On the final day at the railway station, with just minutes before my train left, I finally plucked up the courage to propose. She accepted immediately and I had never felt so happy. I loved this woman so much, I couldn't believe she felt the same way and that we would be able to spend the rest of our lives together.

Since knowing Anna, I finally started leaving my room, which was difficult for me. It had always been my place of safety, where I could hide from the world. The toughest part of all though was discovering that because I had effectively lived on my own for so long, I had become inflexible and used to living selfishly. Fortunately Anna's patience and understanding are remarkable and now, although I occasionally still feel the need to hide from the world, it is lessening with time.

I was also becoming far more comfortable with physical contact, which was new to me. I'd assumed people didn't want me near them and would be repelled if I approached them physically. Now my closeness to Anna was making me feel more comfortable. I had regained my sense of touch and it felt wonderful. The subject of sex was still difficult for both of us. I felt ashamed of being so inexperienced at such a late age and hid my feelings on the subject.

Anna's enthusiasm and encouragement over my script writing led me to re-join a film producer's society. Before long, a small production company told me they liked my work and commissioned me to write some scripts.

My years spent in isolation allowed my feelings of self-hatred to build. Anna had also spent much of her life hiding and despised her own appearance even more strongly. By slowly supporting each other, we grew more comfortable about ourselves physically. It was a few months before we had the courage to sleep together, and we were both so amazed at how good it felt that we wondered why we'd waited so long.

Anna is the kindest person I have ever met. She is always empathic, warm, thoughtful and funny. Her bravery in overcoming anorexia never fails to astound me, but the fact that she is always so generous with her time and affection, despite her inner pain, is almost incomprehensible. Sometimes when she cries, I can sense the depth of this pain, and it feels as though the tears will never stop.

She has not allowed her Grandmother's abuse to make her bitter, and her continuing belief in the goodness of people is evidence of that. Her kindness and patience have given a new dimension to my life. In the time I have known her, I've seen her flourish - she has grown in confidence and challenges the voice constantly.

My life has changed dramatically since I first exchanged letters with Anna. Thanks to her patience, kindness and support, my self-image has improved beyond recognition and I hope I make Anna feel good about herself too. I am so proud to know Anna and I am so in love with her. I am honoured to have helped Anna to continue winning her battle, one day at a time, against anorexia. Anna's story gives so much hope to so many lonely people everywhere. I love you Anna.

EPILOGUE

That special night of the REM concert is now just a year ago and I have lived the last year in a way I never thought possible. Not only have I become a normal adult woman of 31, engaged to a man she loves, travelling around the country but I have also entered a whirlwind world of editors, fellow authors, television and radio interviews.

Last August I started writing this book. The last twelve months have been frightening, exciting, nerve-wracking and thrilling, too thrilling at times, but through it all I have continued recovering from Anorexia nervosa. To find the courage to write my story, I had to physically distance myself from old familiar surroundings. I had to dig deep to find the courage to travel throughout the U.K., spending time in towns I had never visited before. To other people who holiday in Spain and America, it sounds like nothing, but for me to visit towns like Glasgow, Edinburgh and Blackpool was like making a journey to the other side of the world. As my courage grew, our criss-cross tour across England became great fun and to go night clubbing in Birmingham, play pitch and putt in Manchester or bowling in Bradford was wonderful. Simon used some of his savings to pay for us to live and travel during this time. In all we stayed in over twenty towns throughout the U.K. including Liverpool, Oxford, Brighton, Sheffield, York, Newcastle and Leeds.

Today I am no longer acutely anorexic, though I do still suffer from anorexia and probably always will. Anorexia is like drug addiction or alcoholism - the sufferer is always recovering, never completely healed. But like other people who fight their addictions, for the next twenty-four hours I will fight my anorexia and I will win. For just the next day, I will eat.

I wanted to write this book in the hope that I could help other sufferers of this frightening illness. Getting better is not easy but no matter how far down the ladder you have gone, there is a way up. The battle is worth fighting.

I always felt upset reading of wonderful miracle cures from this difficult and complex illness. Why couldn't I get instantly better too? I wanted to. I was the classic anorexic - I wanted to go to sleep one night ill and wake up the next morning well. I wanted to feel happy and free around food again and I wanted to be rid of my constant abusive internal voice.

Many people die from anorexia. I wanted my book to leave the sufferer feeling hopeful, understanding that they can realistically come through this illness. They can live a happy and fulfilling life again but that the journey will be tough and at many stages along the way they will want to give up.

I also wanted to try to explain to people who have no knowledge of Anorexia nervosa what a crippling illness this is. The sufferer is not a difficult teenager, who gazes at models in magazines and selfishly starves themselves near to death just to be thin, as the incorrect media label of anorexia as 'the slimmer's disease' implies. The sufferer is a person who desperately needs help. They are silently crying out for help in the only way they know how. Something in their lives is terribly wrong. They are in pain and they need support and care. These people need love and attention, not punishment regimes or harsh force feeding treatment. Ignorance about this condition has caused many sufferers tremendous heartache.

Every time I read a book on anorexia, I was searching for an answer to many questions - How do I get myself better? How do I cope with this disease? How do I live normally without resorting to starvation as a way of solving my problems? How do I cope with seeing myself as fat and always wanting to be thin?

I started to discover the answers to these questions when I met Simon and I was shown unconditional love. I can clearly see how much Simon loves me and by trusting him and listening to his voice rather than the destructive anorexic one inside my own head, I have started to form a more realistic picture of my own worth. I thought I was worthless but Simon has shown me I am a very special person. I thought I was ugly but Simon has shown me I am beautiful inside and out. By accepting Simon's love and believing him, I have found the strength to beat my anorexia.

I am not advocating my Simon as a cure for all anorexics. He's not available on national loan. But I am saying that all anorexics need to learn to trust and believe someone who cares about them be it relative, friend, partner or counsellor. Talk honestly to this person about your anorexic feelings and listen to their voice rather than the anorexic voice. The anorexic voice wants to destroy, the person who cares for you wants to heal. I often say to Simon:
"I am fat. I just want to be thin again."
He will say:

"Anna you are thin, you are not fat. That is just the anorexic voice speaking to you."

Who do I believe? If I want to get better I have to believe Simon because he is the one telling the truth.

The anorexic voice has always lied to me and deliberately hurt me. If I listen to the anorexic voice, I will just start back down the road to anorexia again.

Gradually, over time, I started to hear another voice in my head. Along with the anorexic voice, I began to hear a louder voice. Simon's voice.

Trust and love were the keys that opened the doors and started to unlock the anorexia inside of me.

Do Simon and I encounter many problems today?

Of course. Living with a recovering anorexic is not always plain sailing but together we are helping each other. Simon had an illness of his own that, though not anorexia, had similar symptoms - low self-esteem and self-confidence and fear of the adult world. I have helped Simon to grow in confidence and the person who I live with now is different in many ways to the man I first met in London 16 months ago. Simon has also helped me to grow in lots of ways. These are just a few of them:-

Before I met Simon, eating out terrified me. Frightened and unsure of what to order, I would soon be presented with a huge plate of food I couldn't eat. When I eat out with Simon, he orders side dishes and we just share the food. This takes the pressure off me. Not forced to tackle a huge plate of food alone, I eat more by nibbling from each dish.

I have always believed that if something went wrong it was my fault - a typical anorexic thought. Since I've been living with Simon, I've started to realise this isn't the case. I now talk with Simon if I feel he's upset me and he is very proud of the fact that I can do this. It is only because I trust him completely that I can. I know that he will not stop loving me if I get angry and I'm grateful Simon is brave enough to take responsibility for his actions. Naturally it is not always Simon that is in the wrong or is the one that hurts me but he does accept responsibility when he is at fault, which has enabled me to feel it's okay to sometimes feel angry with him.

Another problem anorexics have is that they suffer from 'black and white thinking', something Simon has trouble with as well. 'Black and white' or 'All or nothing' thinking means that if something goes wrong, everything has gone wrong. This causes problems if ever Simon and I have an argument because I automatically think everything's gone wrong and I have to leave. My thinking is:
"Simon's upset and I've caused this to happen. I'm a nuisance and a bad part of his life. I should leave him."
I try to leave, which terrifies Simon, who thinks he's losing me and so becomes extremely depressed. I feel guilty for depressing him and feel more certain I should leave, which depresses him further and so the cycle continues.

With Simon's help, I am learning to fight 'black and white thinking'. I have to understand that his love for me is strong and genuine, and that if something goes wrong we sort it out together. It is not the end of the world. Rash decisions are not necessary. There is a solution to every problem.

Another difficult area for me is clothes shopping. After a gap of ten years, I'm starting to buy clothes from shops again rather than catalogues. This can still be a painful and difficult task. Trying on clothes in changing rooms is tough. I still want to be a size 8 and feel heart broken if I don't always fit into these sizes. I still have a distorted body image and find looking in mirrors quite distressing. Simon wants me to buy new clothes since he knows I have trouble buying special things for myself but he hates to see me distressed. He encourages me by telling me how beautiful he finds my body now that it is healthier and that the anorexic skeleton I once was, was not an attractive woman, but a dangerously ill girl.

Body image is still a problem for me and the books that say, "As soon as you reach a healthier weight all your anorexic feelings will disappear", are misleading and distressing to the sufferer.

Simon still feels distressed if I say I want to be thin and look happy if I lose weight but he does realise it is the anorexic voice that is feeling so pleased. He also knows it's the anorexic voice that wants me to self-harm but this frightens him intensely. I promise him I will never cut myself again but the voice is very powerful and I can't give a cast iron guarantee. But I do assure him that I fight the voice constantly and he can see the progress I am making.

Through Simon, I have met many new people and now have a whole circle of very dear friends. Though I still find it hard to talk to strangers at times, this isn't obvious any more. Simon tells me I shine in company and all his friends took me to their hearts immediately. Seeing their reaction to me has helped to build my self-confidence and their love has also helped me to fight the anorexic voice. I had to be brave enough to come out of my shell and meet people. If Simon had allowed me to always run away and hide, he would have just contributed to me becoming very lonely and sad.

Since we've known each other Simon and I have identified the "I'm fine" syndrome. Simon does want to know when I am feeling sad, or upset and he wants to know why. I always put up protective barriers, trying to look after others by saying I'm fine, even when I'm not. This infuriates and distresses Simon. He cannot help me to solve a problem if he doesn't know what it is. The protective barriers are so misplaced. By trying to shelter Simon from my problems, I only cause him more worry. He goes nearly mad wondering what's caused me to feel so low. Knowing about the problem, even if it hurts to know, is better than not knowing. I am slowly learning to share my troubles with Simon. He is an adult man who can deal with problems, however complex or frightening, and once shared, troubles are more resolvable.

A problem that Simon and I share is self-criticism. Putting ourselves down is counter-productive. It upsets the other person and leads us to try to rescue each other. We are always trying to stop the other person from criticising themselves but have difficulty stopping

ourselves. Our friend Mike also puts himself down a lot
(many people actually do) and we've set up a deal
whereby if we put ourselves down when we're together,
we have to pay a forfeit. This works well as it makes you
think before you slip in a subtle put down.

I hope that by reading a few of the problems Simon and I
encounter because of the anorexia, it will help you to
understand more about the illness.

If I can help you in any way or you just want to write,
email me on Anna@anorectic.fsnet.co.uk

GETTING MARRIED SOON

THE INNOCENT CHILD THAT
STARTED LIKE THIS...

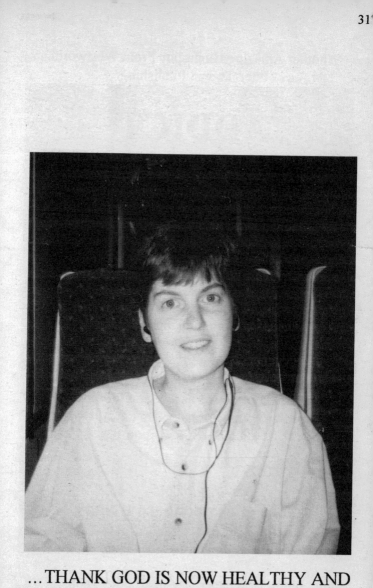

...THANK GOD IS NOW HEALTHY AND
LOOKS LIKE THIS

Another Amazing Biography From Westworld
International Publishing

ADDICT

A true life story by Stephen Smith

Drugs imprisoned me for twenty-six years of my
life. Towards the end of my addiction I lived in shop
doorways on the streets of London.

When all was lost a miracle came along which
enabled me to rejoin the human race. I know of
nobody who slipped so far down for so long and had
the good fortune to come back.

I hope this book serves as a lesson for others and
helps those less fortunate who are still in the
clutches of addiction.

None of us were born tramps.

Addict out now in paperback in all book shops £6.99
ISBN 0-9529215-0-2

ADDICT
AN INCREDIBLE TRUE STORY WITH A FAIRYTALE END
A TWENTY-YEAR DRUG AND DRINK HORROR TRIP FROM RICHES TO INSANITY IN THE GUTTER
IT'S A MIRACLE I LIVED TO WRITE THIS BOOK
STEPHEN SMITH

Slimmer on Trial

You stand in front of the mirror
And survey your lovely figure
You think you're getting fatter
In fact you're getting thinner

The magnifying glass within your eye
Will always blow up the reasons why
The outside world's in constant denial
Always promoting a slimmer on trial

Anorexia world starving yourself
Anorexia world a slim line curse
Anorexia world saying fat is worse
Anorexia world love yourself first

Poem by Robin Munro

robinsrhymes.com